GAME GRAPHICS

THE BEST NEW VIDEO & BOARD GAME DESIGN

ROCKPORT PUBLISHERS • ROCKPORT, MASSACHUSETTS

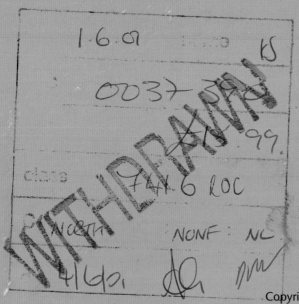

First published in the United States of America by:
Rockport Publishers, Inc.
146 Granite Street
Rockport, Massachusetts 01966
Telephone: (508) 546-9590
Fax: (508) 546-7141

Distributed to the book trade and art trade in the U.S. by:
North Light, an imprint of
F & W Publications
1507 Dana Avenue
Cincinnati, Ohio 45207
Telephone: (513) 531-2222

ISBN 1-56496-079-X

10 9 8 7 6 5 4 3 2 1

Printed in Hong Kong

Book Design
Charles Brunner

Special thanks to Pat and Jennifer Brunner, and Beth and Tom Parker for their support in the design and production of this publication. Special thanks also to Charles Phillips, Jim Engelbrecht, Steve Strumpf, Jim Bremer, Judy Gianareles, Steve Wagner, Steve Peringer, Dave Parmley, Steve Curran, Keith Evans, Brian Balistreri for game and production information.

CONTENTS

4 Introduction

6 Video Games

26 Computer Game Software

56 Handheld & Electronic Games

64 Classic Board Games

90 Adult Games

102 **Children's Board Games**

130 Skill & Action Games

140 Puzzles & Card Games

158 Index

INTRODUCTION

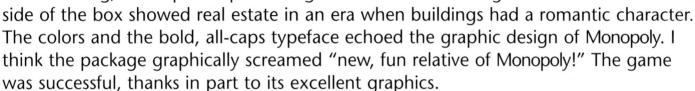

When Parker Brothers decided to produce Advance to Boardwalk, I was delighted. I was also concerned. Since the product was the first spin-off of the incredibly successful Monopoly, its graphics would have to relate to Monopoly, but also be strong enough to convey the new game's personality and stand on their own. This wouldn't be easy.

The final design linked the fun of the beach to the real estate at Boardwalk and the playful character of Uncle Pennybags. The box front featured Monopoly's Rich Uncle Milburn Pennybags, a beach setting, and a periscope looking at a sunbather. The right side of the box showed real estate in an era when buildings had a romantic character. The colors and the bold, all-caps typeface echoed the graphic design of Monopoly. I think the package graphically screamed "new, fun relative of Monopoly!" The game was successful, thanks in part to its excellent graphics.

As a professional game inventor, graphics directly affect my success. In this book you will be treated to graphic applications on games of all kinds: the traditional treatment of classic games; the stylish, up-to-date look of adult games; the whimsical and playfully inviting appearance given to skill and action games; the space-limited treatment of card games; the attention-grabbing look given to video and computer games, and much more. Each game will have its own uniquely different graphics.

Whether your interest is in graphics, games, or simply aesthetics, this book will be of immense interest to you. In the design game, the right graphics can make you a winner.

Charles Phillips

Charles Phillips, a professional game inventor, is a trained mechanical engineer who worked for the Ford Motor Company before pursuing a career in the game industry. He began in a "game think tank", generating 10 game concepts per day. In 1978, after a stint at the Ideal Toy Company, he began inventing games on his own.

His first successful product was I Vant to Bite Your Finger, a vampire game produced by Hasbro©. Many more games followed, including: Advance to Boardwalk, Clue Jr. Detective, Castle Risk, Boggle Bowl, Go For It!, Won Over, Free Parking, Vegas Nites Casino Card Series, Oh Bleep!, and others. He is currently working on a range of games, including some for interactive video.

➤ Chuck Brunner, design director, worked for Parker Brothers, and was responsible for all packaging and game graphics including: Clue, Clue Master Detective, Monopoly, Advance to Boardwalk, Trivial Pursuit, Pente, Q-Bert, Risk, Boggle, Mad Magazine Board and Card Games, Frogger, Merlin, Stop Thief, and Nerf Products.

In 1990, he founded Charles R. Brunner Design, a game graphic design consultant firm. He has worked on projects for Texas Instruments, Rykodisc USA, Brookfield Athletic Company, Western Publishing, Velcro USA, Global Paper & Plastics, and Puffin Marine.

MONOPOLY®
SEGA™
Company
Parker Brothers
Art Director
Jim Engelbrecht
Illustrator
John Hamagami

The use of a traditional illustration was a conscious choice to best illustrate Monopoly and Rich Uncle Pennybags — and to give the package new dimension and to set it apart from the traditional board game.

MONOPOLY® and the game board design are Tonka Corporation's registered trademarks for its real estate trading game and game equipment.

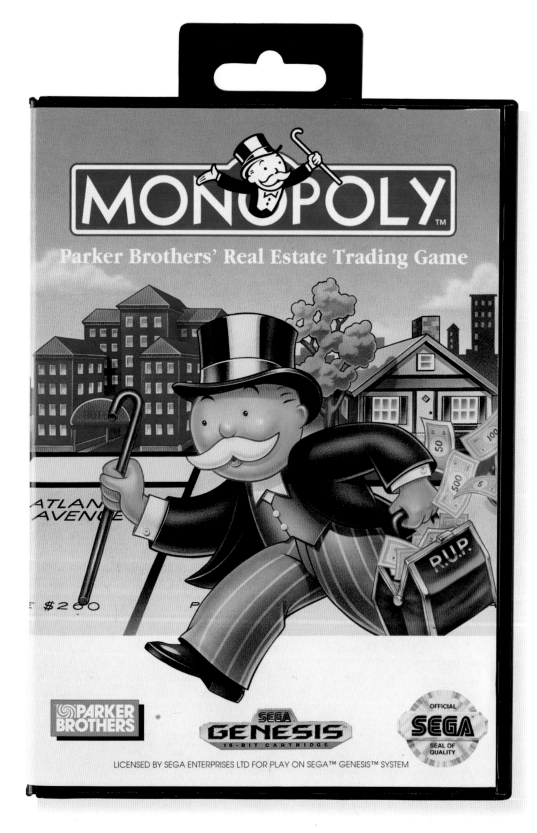

JURASSIC PARK™
Company
Ocean of America, Inc.
Art Director
Jon Beard, Alan Pashley, Steve Kerry
Designer
**Chris Kerry, Jon Beard, Paul Robinson,
Mark Rogers**
Illustrator
John Beard, Alan Pashley, Steve Kerry

The first 3-D textured Super Nintendo game
on the market.

NORTH AND SOUTH™
Company
Kemco Sieka
Design Firm
Josh Freeman
Art Director
Dan Cook
Illustrator
Stephen Peringer

Cover airbrush illustration with Prismacolor
pencil details.

Objective
Build a rich and powerful railway to advance
your armies. Increase troop strength and
cannon power. Amass cavalry. Your combat
prowess and brilliant strategy could rewrite
history on the final battlegrounds of...**NORTH
AND SOUTH.**

BATTLECLASH™
Company
Nintendo of America
Design Firm
Tim Girvin Design
Art Director
Kevin Henderson
Illustrator
Stephen Peringer

Cover airbrush illustration with Prismacolor pencil details.

Objective
The time is the 21st century. In the wake of natural disasters and social unrest, human society has collapsed. The only amusement left for the inhabitants of this grim Earth of the future is the Battle Game. This contest of advanced arena combat pits giant, armored riot suits against each other in a fight to the finish. The winner gains power and prestige, while the loser faces humiliation and dishonor.

© 1992 Nintendo of America, Inc.

8

**JOE & MAC 2:
LOST IN THE TROPICS™**
Company
Data East
Design Firm
Beeline Group
Art Director
Brian Balistreri
Designer
Mary Claire Lee
Illustrator
Greg Winters

Airbrush acrylic and gouache cover illustration. Illustration imported into Adobe Illustrator and assembled in QuarkXPress.

Objective
Our heroes, Joe and Mac, have volunteered to search for their leader's crown and bring it back so that peace can be restored. Of Course, they're not risking their lives just out of the goodness of their hearts — they're out to impress the cave-babes, too! They may have a little problem with navigation. They'd better be careful not to get lost....

©1993 Data East USA, Inc.

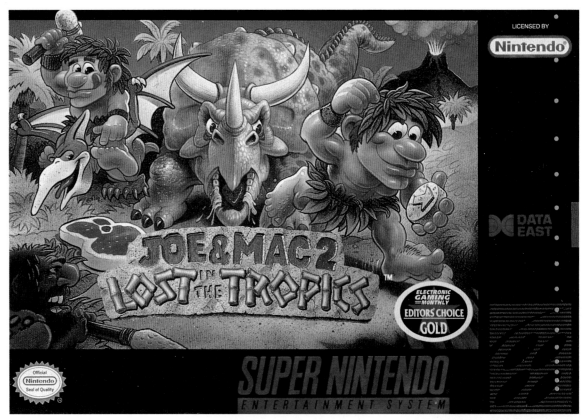

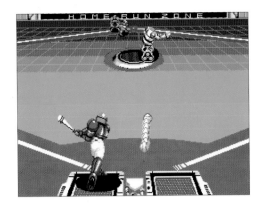

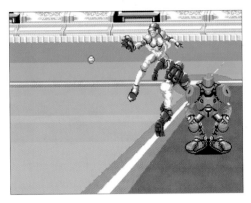

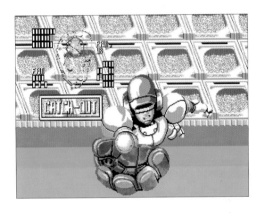

YELLOW JUMP PADS INCREASE JUMPS

FAIR ZONE

2 RED BALL TRAPS STOP THE BALL

SUPER BASEBALL 2020™
Company
Electronic Arts
Design Firm
13th Floor
Art Director
Nancy Fong, Nancy Waisanen
Designer
Dave Parmley
Illustrator
Marc Ericksen

Package graphics designed to
emphasize the speed and fast
action of the smash hit arcade
game. Airbrush cover illustration
was scanned into a Macintosh
Computer and manipulated in
Adobe Photoshop. Baseball
illustration was created in
Photoshop. Package graphics
and type were assembled
in Quark.

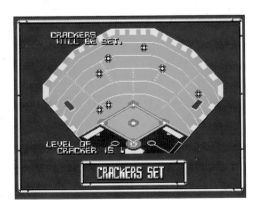

CRACKERS
WILL BE SET.

LEVEL OF
CRACKER IS 1

CRACKERS SET

**SUPER NES PLAY
ACTION FOOTBALL™**
Company
Nintendo of America
Design Firm
Tim Girvin Design
Art Director
Theresa Axe
Designer
Anton Kimble
Illustrator
Stephen Peringer

Cover airbrush illustration
with Prismacolor pencil
details.

Objective
Choose from up to 32
offensive and 16 defensive
plays, then change your
offense on the fly. The
realistic graphics feature
a close-up on the action
and a radar view of the
entire field.

STREET COMBAT™
Company
Irem America Corp.
Design Firm
Image Ink
Art Director
Darlene Kindler
Illustrator
Stephen Peringer

Cover airbrush illustration
with Prismacolor pencil
details.

Objective
Seek out and destroy a
group of ruthless villians
who'll stop at nothing to
wipe you off the map. Each
brutal renegade is a wizard
at martial arts and trick
moves. You must battle
six deadly foes until you
confront your greatest
challenge — their master,
the diabolical C.J.

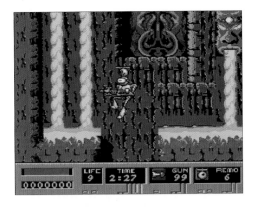

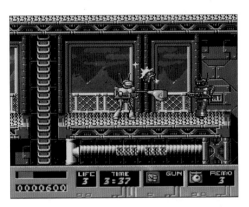

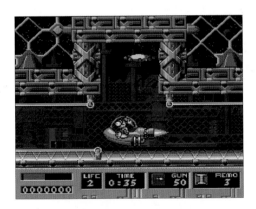

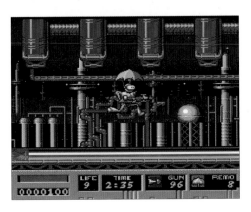

B.O.B.
Company
Electronic Arts
Design Firm
13th Floor
Art Director
Nancy Fong, Nancy Waisanen
Designer
Dave Parmley
Illustrator
Marc Ericksen
Computer Production
Stover Pix

Package graphics feature a friendly super robot hero that breaks the modular border design. Artwork created in Aldus Freehand and Adobe Photoshop. Cover and back graphics and type were assembled in Quark.

RISKY WOODS™
Company
Electronic Arts
Design Firm
13th Floor
Art Director
Nancy Fong, Nancy Waisanen
Designer
Dave Parmley
Computer Production
Matt Hendershot, Stover Pix

Creature illustration was adapted from United Kingdom
game package. The art was scanned and recreated in
Adobe Photoshop. On the package back the graphics
feature a map created in Adobe Photoshop to add to
the element of adventure. Cover and back graphics and
type were assembled in Quark.

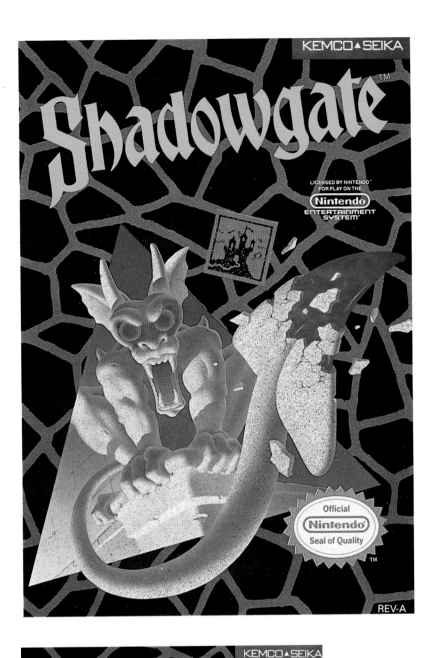

SHADOWGATE™
Company
Kemco Seika
Design Firm
Josh Freeman Associates
Art Director
Greg Clarke
Illustrator
Stephen Peringer

Cover airbrush illustration with Prismacolor pencil details.

Objective
Three-dimensional images, unsurpassed graphics and special sound effects unfold as you venture through grave ruins. But beware! Your next move could be your last. Screens and graphics like those in the best interactive PC games make **SHADOWGATE** a challenging, participatory adventure.

DIGGER T. ROCK™,
Nintendo
Company
Milton Bradley
Art Director
Nan Finkenaur
Designer
Nan Finkenaur
Illustrator
Jim Talbot

Objective
Dare to dig down to the deepest,
most dangerous cavern and
discover what lies beyond.

Digger T. Rock and The Legend of the Lost City are
trademarks of Rare Ltd. © 1990 Rare Ltd. Licensed
to Milton Bradley Company by Rare Coin It, Inc.
NINTENDO® and NINTENDO ENTERTAINMENT
SYSTEM® are trademarks of Nintendo of America, Inc.
Game Pak (NES-GP) © 1990 Milton Bradley Company.

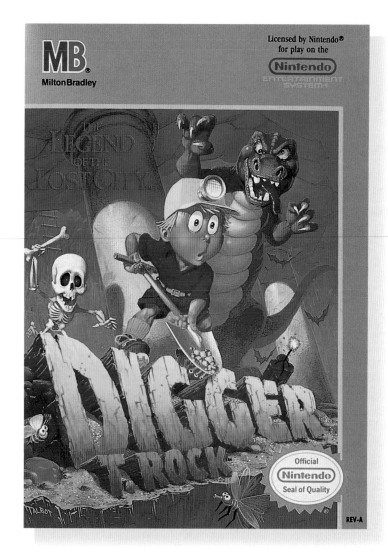

14

THE REN & STIMPY SHOW™:
BUCKEROO$
Company
T•HQ Software
Design Firm
Beeline Group
Art Director
Brian Balistreri
Designer
Steven Wright
Illustrator
George Bates

Cover art — airbrush
acrylic illustration,
scanned into Adobe
Illustrator. Package
assembled in QuarkXpress.

©1993 Nickelodeon. Nickelodeon,
The Ren & Stimpy Show and all
related characters are trademarks owned and
licensed for use by Nickelodeon, a
programming service of Viacom
International, Inc.

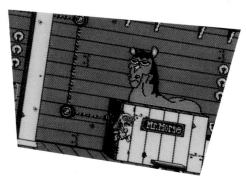

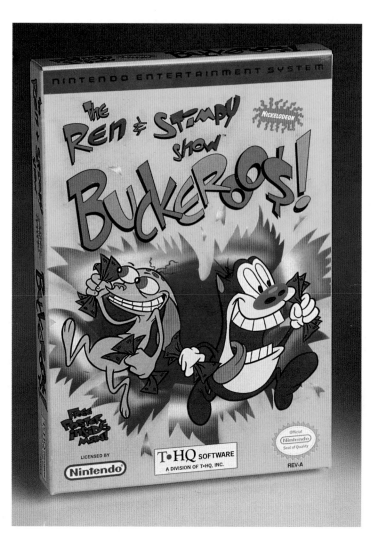

VIDEO GAMES

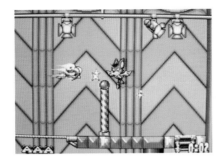

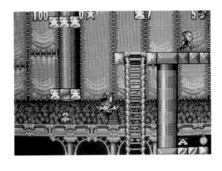

AERO THE ACRO•BAT™
SEGA™
Company
Sunsoft®
Design Firm
Wunderman Cato Johnson

3-D Character was used for box art.

Objective
The madman industrialist Edgar Ektor has seized control of the World of Amusement. He and a deranged cast of fairground freaks threaten the circus. The only hope for survival is the high-flying, death-defying **AERO THE ACRO-BAT**.

THE SHADOW™
Company
Ocean Of America
Programmer
Des Fernando
Artists
Brian Flanagan, Mark Porey, Mathew Wood, Ivan Davies
Musican
Jon Dunn

Building on the popular radio broadcasts and comic books, designers created life-like characters that recreate sequences from the MCA/Universal film. Through use of bright and darker colors as well as fast action movement, the game is loaded with the movie's edge-of-your-seat thrills.

Objective
Gamers enter a shady underworld to save the Big Apple from Genghis Khan's evil descendant. As the game's hero, The Shadow is equipped with unique skills and powers, including cloning and duplicating abilities. Using strategy intensive puzzles as well as good old-fashioned street fighting, players must direct an army of independent agents to reach the game's thrilling climax.

VIDEO GAMES

SUPER SOCCER
Company
Nintendo of America
Design Firm
Tim Girvin Design
Art Director
Theresa Axe
Designer
Anton Kimble
Illustrator
Stephen Peringer

Cover airbrush illustration with Prismacolor pencil details.

Objective
Shoot, pass, dribble and score. **SUPER SOCCER** offers the gut-wrenching intensity and fast action of international soccer competition.

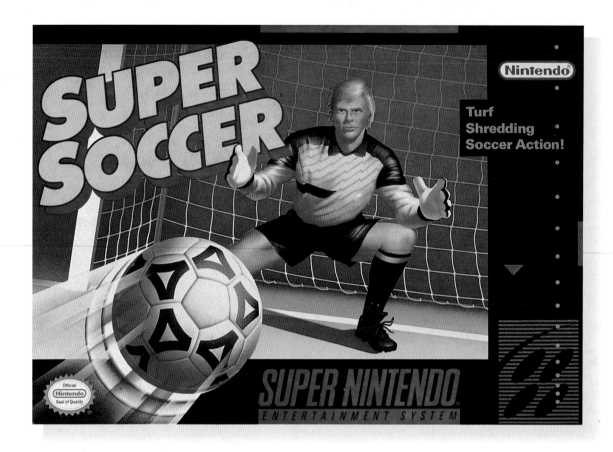

16

DASHIN' DESPERADOES™
Company
Data East
Design Firm
Beeline Group
Art Director
Brian Balistreri
Designer
Lisa Norton
Illustrator
Steve Lang

Characters were sculpted in modeling clay, photographed, and retouched in Adobe Photoshop using a Macintosh Quadra 700.

Objective
Will and Rick, a couple of cool cowdudes, were best friends until Jenny came to town. They've been rivals ever since, competing constantly for her attention. Now Jenny's dad has given her a trip around the world for her birthday. Will and Rick are both determined to go along as her bodyguard — and they'll do anything to top each other! From the deserts of the Southwest to the icebergs of the Arctic, through shark-infested seas and haunted ruins, you'll need your fastest footwork, your wits, and a few handy bombs to keep Jenny safe and sound — and to leave your opponent in the dust! So you'd better get dashin' desperadoes and may the coolest cowdude win!

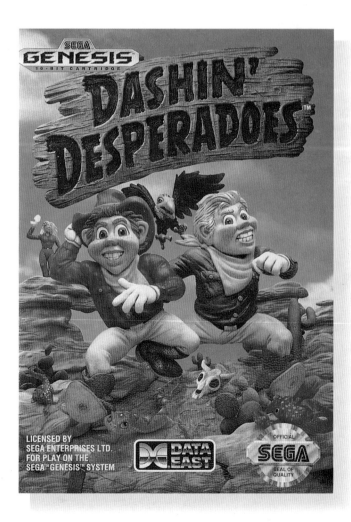

BUGS BUNNY™ RABBIT RAMPAGE,
SUPER NES
Company
Sunsoft
Design Firm
Wunderman Cato Johnson

Objective
Animated exploits abound when
a demented cartoonist "paints" Bugs
Bunny into every perilous predicament
imaginable. Be on the risky end of an
Elmer Fudd "wabbit" hunt. Then "Draw,
pardner!" in a showdown with Yosemite
Sam. But don't flinch. Because the entire
ACME arsenal is at your command.
Exploding dog bones, pies in the face,
loaded paint brushes and more.

NHL® STANLEY CUP®
Company
Nintendo of America
Design Firm
Tim Girvin Design
Art Director
Steven Panone
Illustrator
Stephen Peringer

Cover airbrush illustration
with Prismacolor pencil details.

Objective
NHL STANLEY CUP's unique, super-
realistic, three-dimensional viewpoint
on the action puts you in center ice,
always on the puck, always in the play.

VIDEO GAMES

DÉJÀ VU™
Company
Kemco Seika
Design Firm
Josh Freeman Associates
Art Director
Dan Cook
Illustrator
Stephen Peringer

Cover airbrush illustration with Prismacolor pencil details.

Objective
Search through a seedy Chicago casino — decorated with one somewhat familiar but very dead body. Find out who you are and who iced this guy. Deja Vu. In this case, what you don't know can kill you.

Déjà Vu, A Nightmare Comes True™ is a trademark of KOM Simulations, Inc. and is used with permission.

THE BUGS BUNNY™
CRAZY CASTLE
Company
Kemco Seika
Design Firm
Josh Freeman Associates
Art Director
Greg Clarke
Illustrator
Stephen Peringer

Cover airbrush illustration with Prismacolor pencil details.

Objective
With a deft wrist, a quick wit, and a swift kick, you will win the game and have Bugs and Honey hopping happily together again.

© 1989 Kemco.

METAL COMBAT™
Company
Nintendo of America
Design Firm
Tim Girvin Design
Art Director
Steven Panone
Illustrator
Stephen Peringer

Cover airbrush illustration with Prismacolor pencil details.

™ and ® are trademarks of Nintendo of America Inc. ©1993 Nintendo of America Inc.

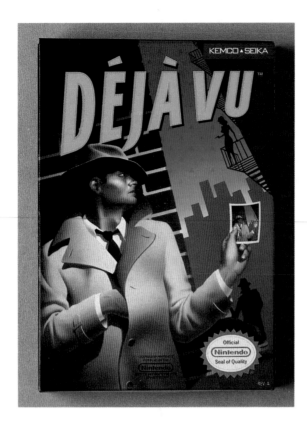

VIDEO GAMES

CONGO'S CAPER
Company
Data East
Design Firm
Beeline Group
Art Director
Brian Balistreri
Designer
Lisa Norton
Illustrator
Steve Lang

Cover illustration created
using acrylics. Package
assembled in QuarkXPress.

Objective
If you were a monkey, just hangin'
out in the jungle with your chimp-
chick, and a magic ruby fell out of
the sky and zapped you both,
turning you into half humans, and
a demon-kid swooped down and
made off with your girl what
would you do? You'd stop at
nothing to save her, that's what.
Your search for little Congette will
take you from ghost towns to
pirate ships to ninja castles to the
belly of a Tyrannosaurus.

© 1992 Data East USA, Inc.

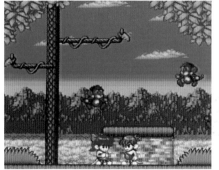 

19

**THE DEATH AND RETURN OF
SUPERMAN™**
Company
Sunsoft®
Design Firm
Wunderman Cato Johnson

VIDEO GAMES

**THE REN & STIMPY SHOW™:
VEEDIOTS!**
Company
T•HQ Software
Design Firm
Beeline Group
Art Director
Brian Balistreri
Designer
Steven Wright
Illustrator
George Bates

Cover art - airbrush acrylic
illustration, scanned into Adobe
Illustrator. Package assembled in
Quark Express.

20

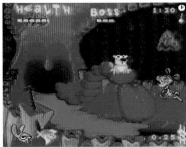 

SUPER R-TYPE®
Company
Irem America Corp.
Design Firm
Image Ink
Art Director
Darlene Kindler
Illustrator
Stephen Peringer

Airbrush Illustration, details added in
Prismacolor Pencils.

**DAFFY DUCK™
THE MARVIN MISSIONS**
Company
Sunsoft®
Design Firm
Wunderman Cato Johnson

Objective
Get ready to duck and cover, because the fate of the planet rests squarely on Duck Dodgers — Alias Daffy Duck — the fearless space crusader from the cartoon adventure series.

**JURASSIC PARK II™,
SUPER NES**
Company
Ocean®
Design Firm
Ocean®
Programmers
**Bobby Earl, David Chiles,
Dean Evans**
Artists
**Jack Wikeley, John Lomax,
Ged Grainger, Ilyas Kadvji,
Richard Heasman, Craig Whittle**
Musician
Dean Evans

In non-stop 3-D action, this game's 16 levels of excitement were created with Mode 7 graphics customized to the Super NES platform. Designers created this exciting and powerful game, using actual digitized sound effects from the film, along with true-to-life renderings of the movie's famous characters.

GUNFORCE™
Company
Irem America Corp.
Design Firm
Image Ink
Art Director
Darlene Kindler
Illustrator
Stephen Peringer

Cover airbrush illustration with
Prismacolor pencil details.

©1992 Irem America Corp.

TOTAL CARNAGE™
Company
Malibu Games
Design Firm
Beeline Group
Art Director
Brian Balistreri
Designer
Steven Wright
Illustrator
David McMacken

Cover illustrated in oil.

Total Carnage™ is a trademark of and licensed from
Midway® Mfg. Co., ©1992 All Rights Reserved.

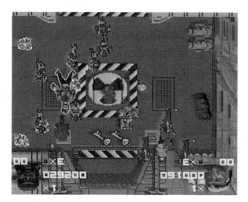

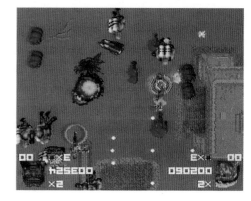

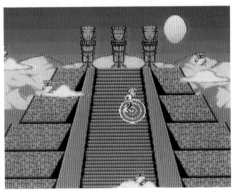

MIGHTY MAX™
Genesis™
Company
Ocean®
Design Firm
WJS Design
Art Director
WJS Design

Characters are taken directly from the hit cartoon series. Innovative two-player split-screen mode allows for cooperative or head-to-head play.

Objective
Mighty Max pits gamers against the evil SkullMaster in 50 levels of puzzles, action, and time-travelling adventures. Gamers must travel through time and space while fighting off and avoiding the SkullMaster.

EEK! THE CAT™
Company
Ocean®
Design Firm
Ocean®
Art Director
Richard Creek
Programmer
John Scott
Musician
Keith Tinman

VIDEO GAMES

THE FLINTSTONES®
Genesis™
Company
Ocean®
Design Firm
Ocean
Art Director
Adrian Ludley, Alan Pashley
Programmer
Mark Rogers, Paul Robinson
Illustrator
Steve Kerry, Bart McLaughlin

The design captures the distinct look and feel of the film through the use of actual sound bites from the movie, and true character likenesses of all the stars. The cartoon quality graphics and animation, and the many levels of deep and diverse gaming make this colorful game fun for the whole family.

Objective
Gamers play in a cartoon world filled with stunning graphics, hilarious animation sequences, and all the movie's zany characters and icons. The objective is to lead Fred Flintstone through 45 levels of danger, dinosaurs, and jungle.

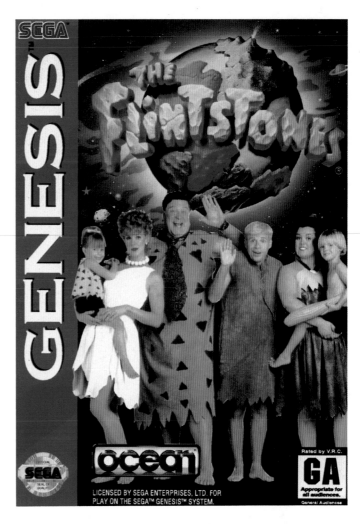

24

ADDAMS FAMILY® **VALUES**
Company
Ocean®
Design Firm
Ocean
Art Director
**Don McDermott,
John Hackleton**
Programmer
**Rob Walker, Phil Trelford,
John May, David Chiles**
Musician
Keith Tinman

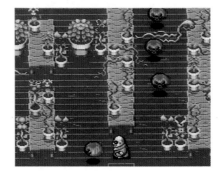

BIMINI RUN™
Company
Nuvision Entertainment
Design Firm
Charles R. Brunner
Design
Art Director
Chuck Brunner
Designer
Russ Richter
Illustrator
Jeff Stock
Screen Graphics
Sam Kjellman
Programmer
Micro Smith, Inc., Rex Bradford, Charlie Heath, Mark Lesser, Richard Blewett

Cover airbrush illustration with Prismacolor pencil details.

Objective
Prepare yourself. This is no joy ride. You'll need every bit of skill and cunning you have. And something more: You'll also need luck. Because nothing is quite as it seems in the **BIMINI ZONE**.

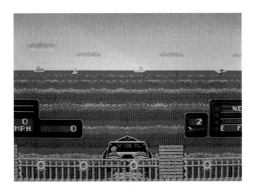

HEY JAZZ FISH!
Company
Green Arts Entertainment
Design Firm
Howie Green Design
All Design
Howie Green
Illustrator
Howie Green, Chris Lowery

The cursor is also an animated
cursor character. CD-Rom activity game.

RETURN OF THE PHANTOM™
Company
Microprose Software
Design Firm
Microprose Software
Designer
Kenn Nishuye, Frank Fraizer, Anne Jennifer Walker
Illustrator
Kenn Nishuye, Frank Fraizer, Anne Jennifer Walker

Graphics for animated graphic adventures were hand painted, then scanned and touched up.

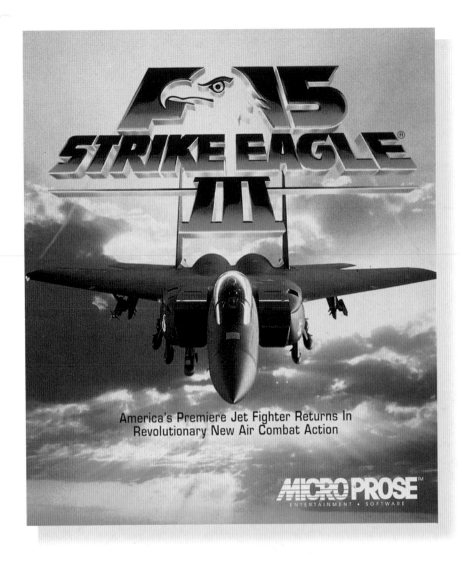

F-15 STRIKE EAGLE III
Company
Microprose Software
Design Firm
Microprose Software
All Design
Barbara Bents Miller
Frank Vivirito

All Art © Microprose 1994.

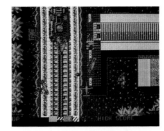

SKY SHARK™
Company
Taito
Design Firm
Qually & Company, Inc.
Art Director
Robert Qually
Desiger
Robert Qually, Karla Walusiak, Holly Thomas, Charles Senties
Illustration
Don Kusker

The authentic design of a P-40 plane, along with Air Force pilot's wings, bring the gamer back in history. The screen shots use brighter color combinations, giving the game an optimistic, more inspirational feel than other, more ominous games.

Objective
SKY SHARK takes its players into a full force, World War II battle in the skies. Gamers are the Shark, the best pilot in the squadron, and must enter into enemy territory to save a fallen group of airmen from a terrible fate.

Taito® and Sky Shark® are trademarks of Taito America Corporation. Copyright © 1989.

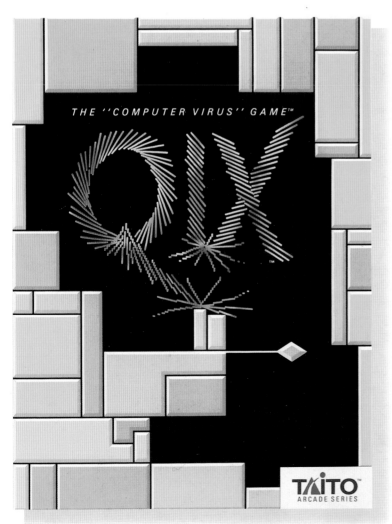

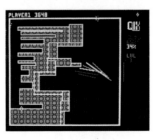

QIX™
Company
Taito
Design Firm
Qually & Company, Inc.
Art Director
Robert Qually
Designer
Robert Qually , Karla Walusiak, Holly Thomas, Charles Senties
Illustration
Ron Villani

This game's original form is the rectangular box shape, not an album shape as with other packages. The Qix is represented by a rainbow helix that actually spells out QIX in its shape. The use of fluorescent colors on a black screen gives a spontaneous look to the image, while the Qix-trapping squares made with rubylithe-type film on acetate bring the rainbow helix to life.

Taito® and QIX® are trademarks of Taito America Corporation. Copyright © 1989.

COMPUTER GAME SOFTWARE

System Requirements
Requires a 256-color-capable Macintosh II family computer with a 13" or larger color monitor, System 6.07 or later, at least 8 Megabytes of RAM, a multimedia compatible CD-ROM drive, and QuickTime version 1.5 (included).

Published by Presto Studios, Inc., P.O. Box 262535, San Diego, CA 92196-2535 619-689-4895

©1992 Presto Studios, Inc. All rights reserved. Apple, Macintosh, and QuickTime are trademarks of Apple Computer, Inc., registered in the U.S. and other countries

You walk hesitantly down the poorly lit corridor. "This could be the end of me," you think, "it could all end right here, and humanity would suffer for a thousand generations because of my failure." As you reach the corner, you are faced with a weighty decision: risk your life in defense of all that man has achieved in the past several hundred years, or turn safely back to a future marred in ways that only you will ever know. You turn, and suddenly you are caught frozen in the steely gaze of your worst nightmare, a seven foot tall alloy beast with one purpose and no heart, and only you are standing in its way...

The year is 2318. The unified world is finally at peace. But now, what took centuries to achieve could be instantly unraveled by the power of time travel. You are a member of the Temporal Protectorate, an elite group of agents whose sole purpose is to safeguard history from sabotage. It is during your usual shift at the Temporal Security Annex when the warning alarms suddenly sound; a rip has been detected in the fabric of time. Only moments remain until the continuum is changed forever. Your objective—jump back in time and prevent the corruption from ever happening! But before the game is over, you will have to discover the source of this mayhem and bring it

Take a ride through time — from the prehistoric past to the worlds of the future!

- Photorealistic 3D worlds which can be fully explored.
- A branching story line as sophisticated as any feature film.
- Over 30 minutes of QuickTime video shot with professional actors, featuring Graham Jarvis, who guest starred in the "Unification" episode of **Star Trek: The Next Generation.**
- A totally original music score.
- A hi-fi version of THE JOURNEYMAN PROJECT™ soundtrack is included on the disc so you can listen to it on any conventional stereo CD player.
- Integrated arcade and mind games to challenge any player.

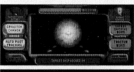

- An intuitive interface featuring easy-to-use inventory and movement controls, helpful information windows, and an expandable BioChip panel.
- THE JOURNEYMAN PROJECT is non-linear. There is no set order in which the goals must be accomplished, and more than one solution exists for each problem that you encounter.

Play the game that will change history: The Journeyman Project!

THE JOURNEYMAN PROJECT™
Company
Presto Studios, Inc.
Art Director
Jack Davis
Designer
Jill Davis

THE JOURNEYMAN PROJECT is the first photorealistic CD-ROM adventure game for Macintosh computers.

31

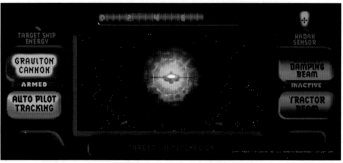

the HUMANS™
Insult to Injury
80 Masochistic Add-On Levels

Think back, way back to that first day that you saw THE HUMANS on the shelf. "Oh yes," you might have said aloud; "oh yes, I will own you, I will tame you, I will break your spirit, I will master you, and yes, oh yes...I promise you...victory will be mine." You took the product home, your hands trembled as you tore off the shrinkwrap, and beads of sweat formed on your upper lip in anticipation... and fear. One week later and where was the game? Tossed into the slag heap of all the other software titles you had crushed, used and degraded. But like a greek tragedy here you are again, faced with eighty tougher, stronger, bitter, human levels. Your head is swimming with nostalgia, and your hands, they're...trembling. Go ahead, buy it...you know you want it.

YOU MUST OWN THIS.

GAMETEK

©1992 Atari Corporation, Licensed to Imagitec, Inc.. Sublicensed to Gametek., All Rights Reserved.
Packaging © 1992 Gametek, Inc. Produced by Imagitec Design, Inc. Humans is a trademark of Gametek, Inc
2999 N.E. 191st Street, Suite 500, North Miami Beach, Fl 33180 U.S.A.

0 43948 00219 4

SMILE

Despite the fact that Insult to Injury contains a generous helping of an indignity and death, the installation of this product is really quite pain. So relax, follow the instructions below.

NOTE: These new levels will REPLACE the original levels. To play the original levels reinstall your original Humans game.

INSERT DISK 1 INTO YOUR DISK DRIVE.

TYPE A: (or the applicable drive letter) TYPE HDINST C (or whatever hard drive your HUMANS game resides on).

GAME WILL NOW UPDATE YOUR HUMANS GAME WITH 80 BRAND LEVELS.

HUMANS AS NORMAL. ALL OF THE PASSWORDS WILL BE NEW EXCEPT FIRST LEVEL, WHICH IS ALWAYS "DARWIN"

Tip Line: 1-900-903-GAME (4963)
charge.
ne required
st have parental permission before calling
ble 24 hours

Customer Service: 1-305-935-3995
◆ 8 a.m. to 8 p.m., Eastern time

Free Introductory CompuServe Membership

As a valued Gametek customer, you are eligible for a special offer to receive a FREE introductory membership to CompuServe — the world's largest on-line information service.

By joining CompuServe, you can receive the latest news and product announcements concerning Gametek games. From the Game Publishers Forum [GO GAMEPUB], you can download updates to your favorite computer games or obtain demos of soon-to-be-released computer and cartridge game players in be able to trade tips, hints and strategies with other Gametek computer and cartridge game players in the Gamers Forum [GO GAMERS].

To take advantage of this special offer, call toll-free 1-800-524-3388 and ask for Representative # 436 to get your introductory CompuServe membership which includes a personal User ID, password, $15 usage credit and an entire month's worth of basic services free.

©1993 Atari Corporation, licensed to Imagitec Design Inc., sublicensed to Gametek, Inc., All Rights Reserved. ©1993 Imagitec Design, Inc.
Humans is a trademark of Gametek, Inc. 2999 N.E. 191st Street, Suite 500, N. Miami Beach, Florida 33180. U.S.A.

KICK ME

---

the HUMANS™
IBM/Tandy & 100% Compatibles
640K VGA only
DATA DISK #2
High Density

the HUMANS™
IBM/Tandy & 100% Compatibles
640K VGA only
DATA DISK #1
High Density
GAMETEK

© 1992 Atari Corporation, licensed to Imagitec Design, Inc., sublicensed to Gametek, Inc. All rights reserved. Packaging © 1992 Gametek, Inc. Humans is a trademark of Gametek, Inc. Produced by Imagitec Design, Inc. 2999 N.E. 191st Street, Suite 500, North Miami Beach, Fl 33180

**THE HUMANS —
INSULT TO INJURY**
Company
Gametek, Inc.
Design Firm
Gametek Creative
Art Director
Stephen Curran
Designer
John Tombley
Illustrator
Elwood Smith

Pen and ink cover illustration was
imported into Adobe Photoshop,
then the images were refined in
Adobe Illustrator, Aldus Freehand
and assembled in QuarkXPress.

**COMPUTER
GAME SOFTWARE**

DRAGONSPHERE
Company
Microprose Software
Design Firm
Microprose Software
All Design
**Bob Kathman,
Mike Gibson**

Graphics for animated
graphic adventures were
hand painted, then
scanned and touched up.

All Artwork ©Microprose Software 1994

RENEGADE™
Company
Taito
Design Firm
Qually & Company, Inc.
Art Director
Robert Qually
Design
**Robert Qually, Karla Walusiak,
Holly Thomas, Charles Senties**
Illustrator
Ron Villani

Recognizable characters, and
uncomplicated levels objectives are easily
related to comic book super-heroes and
storylines. Simple illustration techniques
support the "good vs. evil" theme.

Objective
This is a fast-paced, real life, street-style
karate action game. The story line
involves a man alone in the subway
who encounters various gang members.
Gamers must fight off these enemies as
they approach with pipes, chains, and
their fists.

Taito® and Renegade® are trademarks of Taito
America Corporation. Copyright © 1989.

**COMPUTER
GAME SOFTWARE**

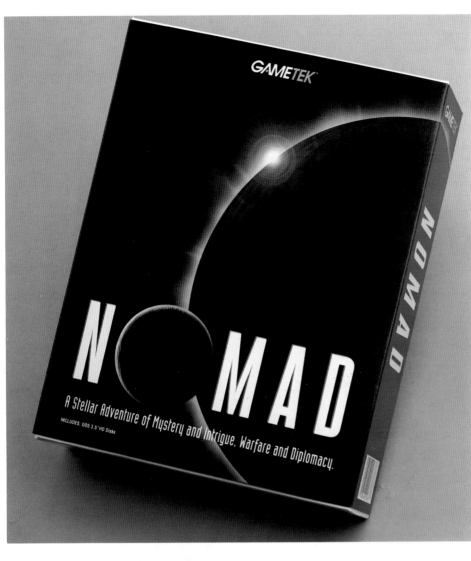

NOMAD™
Company
Gametek, Inc.
Design Firm
Gametek Creative
Art Director
Stephen Curran
Designer
John Tombley
Illustrator
Tim Alt

The cover image is a composite photograph that was recreated in Adobe Photoshop. The package images were assembled in Aldus Freehand and QuarkXPress. When the image was being created a wrong key was accidentally touched changing the color. This happy accident changed the color direction of the final art.

Nomad and Papyrus are trademarks of Papyrus Design Group, Inc.

PIRATES! GOLD®
Company
Microprose Software
Art Director
Michael Haire
All Design
Michael Haire
Chris Soares

This is the first Microprose game using Super VGA Graphics.

Objective
Lead a crew of hot-blooded buccaneers into rollicking harbor towns. And risk your booty and your life plundering enemy ships!

All graphics ©Microprose 1994.

**NOODLE GOES TO
THE HOSPITAL**
Company
The Board/Chicago
Design Firm
Howie Green Design
All Design
Howie Green
Illustrator
**Howie Green,
Christopher Lowery**

This game features screens from
a children's educational video
game called *Noodle Goes to the
Hospital.* The game is designed to
alleviate children's fear of hospitals,
and can be customized to fit
different locations.

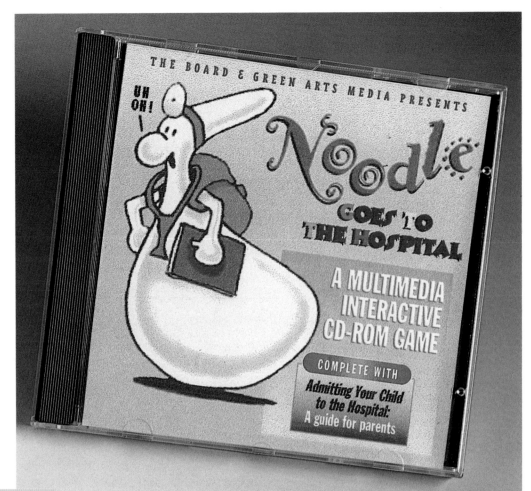

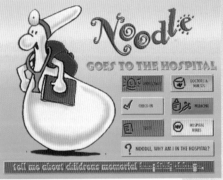

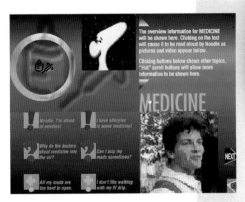

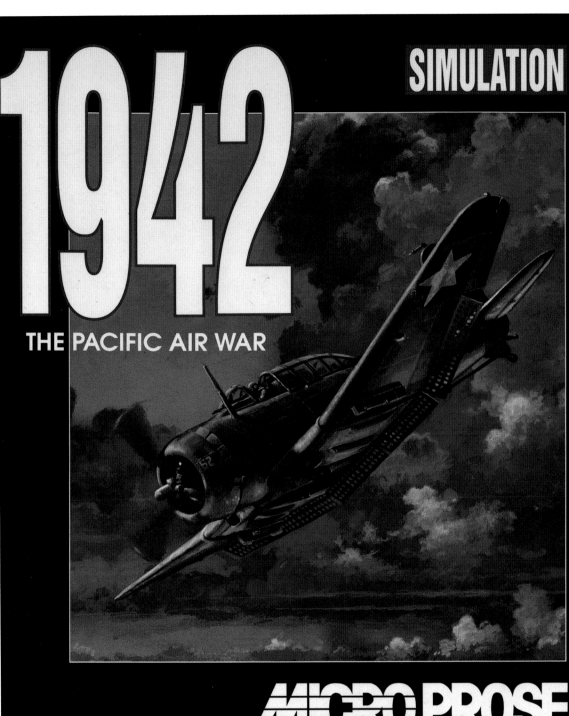

1942: THE PACIFIC AIR WAR
Company
Microprose Software
All Design
**Michael Bates,
Andy Laken, Todd Brizzi,
Max D. Remington III**

This cover illlustration is an acrylic painting. The screen graphics were rendered with Autodesk 3D Studio Modeling Tool. The single plane is an example of Microprose Real-Time 3D game graphics, built with an in-house tool.

All Art © Microprose 1994.

39

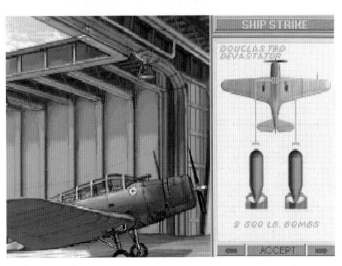

**COMPUTER
GAME SOFTWARE**

ALCON™

Company
Taito
Design Firm
Qually & Company, Inc.
Art Director
Robert Qually
Design
**Robert Qually, Karla Walusiak,
Holly Thomas, Charles Senties**

This simple and clean, yet futuristic game was created through pen and ink illustration and photo-images. Special effects such as abstract paintings, colored lights, and electronic microscopic photographs, helped to form the planet, city, and foreground design.

Objective
The Allied League of Cosmic Nations choose the gamer to pilot the top secret SW475 Starfighter in order to stop the alien occupation of the planet, Orac. To reclaim the planet, gamers must destroy the alien enemy once and for all.

40

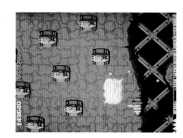  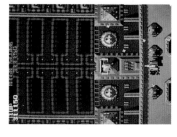

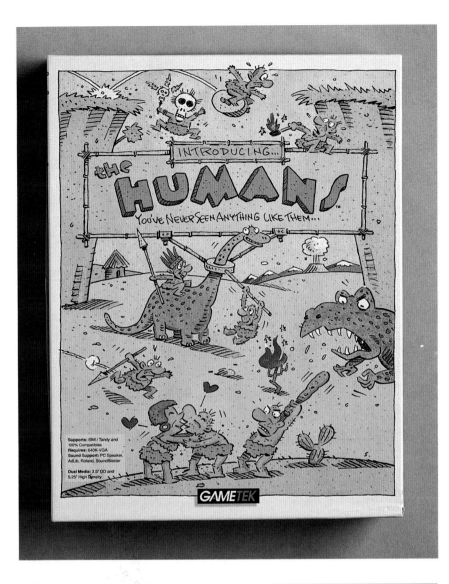

THE HUMANS
Company
Gametek, Inc.
Design Firm
Gametek Creative
Art Director
Stephen Curran
Designer
John Tombley
Illustrator
Elwood Smith

Pen and ink cover illustration was imported into Adobe Photoshop, then the images were refined in Adobe Illustrator, Aldus Freehand and assembled in QuarkXPress.

Objective
It's a naive struggle against extinction, where players score points by finishing levels with as many tribesmen intact as is HUMAN-ly possible. Love, death, food...it's all here.

**COMPUTER
GAME SOFTWARE**

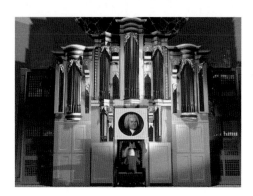

C.P.U. BACH
Company
Microprose
Art Director
Michael Haire
Designer
Michael Haire, Chris Soares
Illustrator
**Chris Soares, Michael Haire,
Barbara Bents Miller,
Nick Rusko-Berger**

Graphic images are a combination of 2-D and 3-D art. Built for 3DO using 3-D Studio.

**COMPUTER
GAME SOFTWARE**

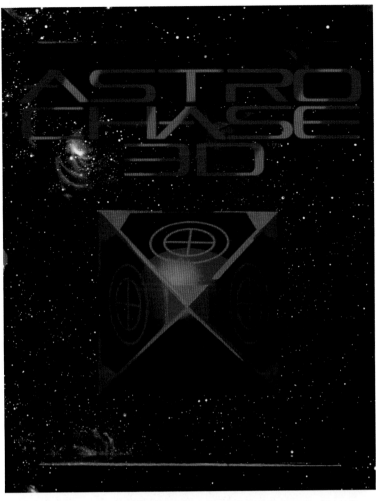

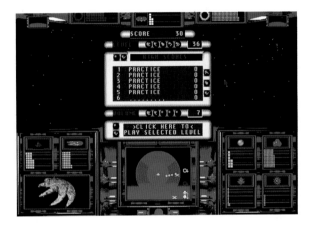

ASTRO CHASE 3D™
Company
**Macplay,
A Division of Interplay Productions**
Design Firm
Macplay/Georgopolous
Art Director
Jane Gilbertson
Designer
Larry Fukouka

An interesting box supports the theme of the title and sells itself to the retailers. (Who do not like odd shaped boxes.)

Objective
Fly into the **ASTRO CHASE-3D™** galaxy as Commander of Ultraship technology. Single Thrust Propulsion™ allows you to lock on course while simultaneously shooting in any direction. The Software Accelerator Graphics Engine18 (S.A.G.E.)™ manipulates graphics with such speed and memory efficiency that it can render highly detailed, lifelike environments in real time...resulting in a new level of gameplay intensity.

43

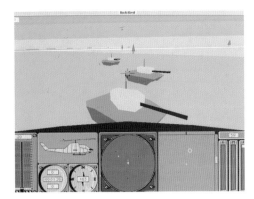

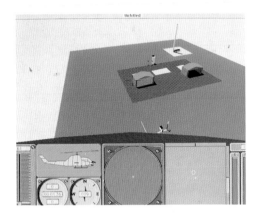

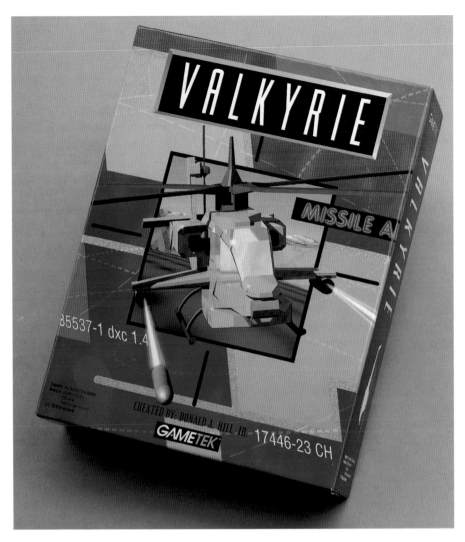

VALKYRIE™
Company
Gametek, Inc.
Design Firm
Gametek Creative
Art Director
Stephen Curran
Designer
John Tombley
Illustrator
Tim Alt

Cover art created in Adobe Photoshop and assembled in Aldus Freehand.

Objective
VALKYRIE greatly simplifies flying, allowing players to concentrate on threat detection, target acquisition, enemy destruction, hitting targets, and accomplishing the mission.

Valkyrie is a trademark of Gametek, Inc.

SID MEIER'S CIVIL WAR™
Company
Microprose Software
Designer
Microprose Software
Art Director
Barbara Bents Miller
Illustrator
Barbara Bents Miller,

All Art © Microprose 1994.

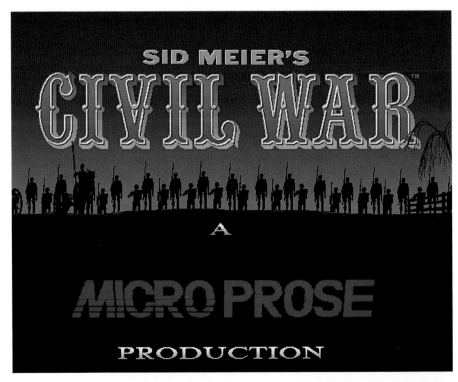

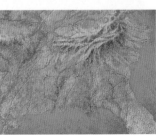

PROPHECY: VIKING CHILD™
Company
Gametek, Inc.
Design Firm
Gametek, Inc.
Art Director
Stephen Curran
Illustrator
David Moses

The cover is an airbrush acrylic illustration with details added in color pencils, refined in Aldus Freehand and assembled in QuarkXPress. The title logo is foil stamped and embossed.

Objective
Welcome to Odin's World. It is a land full of good and evil, within which you must become Brian, The Viking Child, whose heroics have been foretold by the prophets. But there's trouble in the land where you live...Your family and friends are being held on the astral plane, imprisoned by the forces of darkness.

As Brian, your adventure will take you through many beautiful but dangerous places, where you will encounter great adversaries. Among these will be the eight apprentices of evil, slaves to the Dark Lord Loki, who will force you to fight or question your purpose under threat of punishment or penalty.

LAUGH FACTORY
Company
Green Arts Entertainment
Design Firm
Howie Green Design
All Design
Howie Green
Illustrator
**Christopher Lowery,
Howie Green**

The CD-rom based game is
designed to be silly fun for a
PG audience.

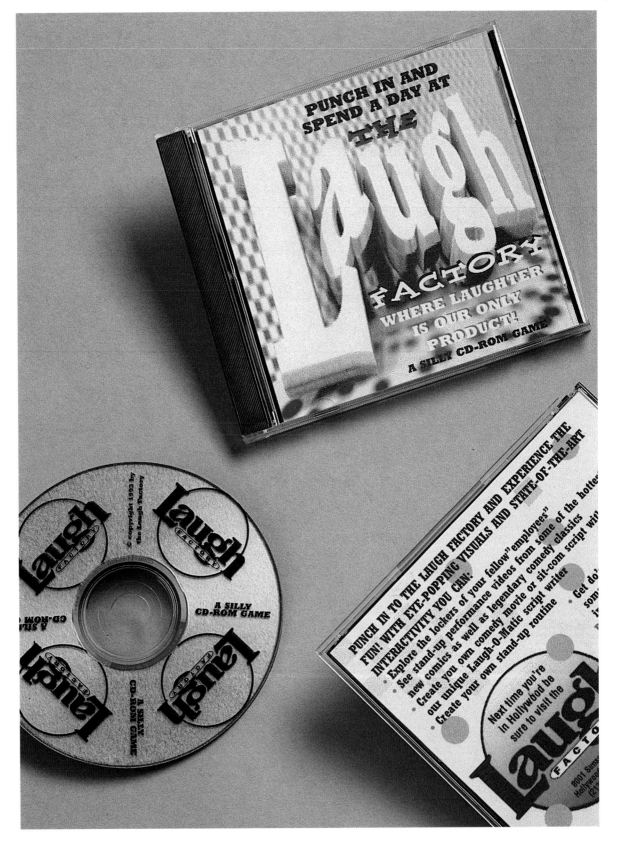

100% GUARANTEED BRAINLESS FUN!

MAC ATTACK

Supports: System 7.0 or higher
Black/White, Grayscale, and Color Monitors
All Screen Sizes
Memory: 2 MEG memory for B&W, 4 MEG memory for Color
Hard Drive required
Enclosed: 3.5" High Density Disk Only

GAMETEK

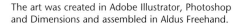

Attention Video Pilot...

The Net, the world's Macintosh super computer network, has been taken over! Someone or something has gained control of the Net by infecting it with viruses that are causing total turmoil. We have isolated your terminal as a primary location to attack these viruses head on in NetSpace, the graphical user-interface of the Net. You must kill all the viruses as you work your way deeper, sector by sector, into the heart of the Net. Your enemies will get tougher and team up on you if you are unable to blow them up quickly. We are counting on you to discover a way to destroy the evil force behind this crisis and restore the Net and the world to order once again. **Good Luck.**

Large screen play, digitized sounds and music, incredible speed and 3-D graphics.

NEW REALITY **GAMETEK**

MAC ATTACK
Company
Gametek, Inc.
Design Firm
Gametek, Inc.
Art Director
Stephen Curran
Designer
David Johnson
Illustrator
Javier Romero Studios

The art was created in Adobe Illustrator, Photoshop and Dimensions and assembled in Aldus Freehand.

Objective
The NEt, the world's Macintosh supercomputer network, has been taken over. Someone or something has gained control of the NEt by infecting it with viruses that are causing total turmoil. We have isolated a primary location to attack these viruses head on. An access to NEtSpace, the graphical user interface of the NEt, has been available to your terminal. We are counting on you to discover a way to destroy this evil force and restore the NEt and the world to order once again.

47

Green Arts Entertainment Presents

MAMBOPAINT

THE INTERACTIVE DIGITAL COLORING BOOK
25 Mamboland pictures to color on screen
or print out and color by hand.
16 colors with 6 different palettes
Featuring Jazz Fish, Noodle and the Gang

MAC version-1 floppy disk will play on any color Macintosh

WOW! THE COLORS! COOL!

Here are 25 of Howie Green's Mamboland pictures to color on your computer screen with 7 different color palettes...or print out black and white versions of each picture and color them by hand. Either way it's hours of coloring fun for kids and slightly goofy adults. This package contains the entire program on one floppy disk... nothing to install. Just pop in the disk, click on the icon and away you go! Look Mom, I'm coloring!

© Copyright 1993 by Howie Green

MAMBOPAINT
Company
Howie Green Design
Design Firm
Howie Green Design
Art Director
Howie Green
Designer
Howie Green, Chris Lowery
Illustrator
Howie Green

*COMPUTER
GAME SOFTWARE*

FLEET DEFENDER™
Company
Microprose Software
Design Firm
Microprose Software
All Design
Terrence Hodge
Max D. Remington III

Real Time 3-D Game Graphics.

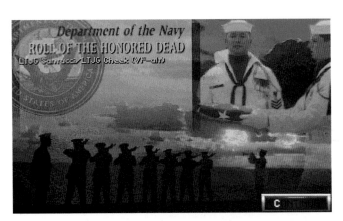

Sid Meier's
CIVILIZATION™

Build An Empire To Stand The Test Of Time

49

We note that your primitive civilization has not achieved bronze working. Perhaps you would care to exchange knowledge with us?
*Buzz off
*OK

SID MEIER'S CIVILIZATION™
Company
Microprose Software
Design Firm
Microprose Software
All Design
Michael Haire

All Art © Microprose 1994.

KING'S TABLE™
Company
Gametek, Inc.
Design Firm
Gametek Creative
Art Director
Stephen Curran
Designer
John Tombley
Photographer
Dominic Marsden

Cover photo based on the ancient European board game "Ragnarok". (Celtic version of Chess.) The shadow figure represents the Odin. Logo produced in pen and ink. Art file was recreated in Adobe Illustrator and assembled in Aldus Freehand.

Objective
The game features 12 different opponents, each with their own personality and style. The dramatic story unfolds with stunning graphics and brilliantly animated sequences. The opponents are a formidable collection of gods from the legendary Valhalla. Play against the computer or a friend. Lose yourself to this faraway world of challenge, intrigue and logic, the table is set...and the gods are waiting.

King's Table is a trademark of Gametek, Inc.

51

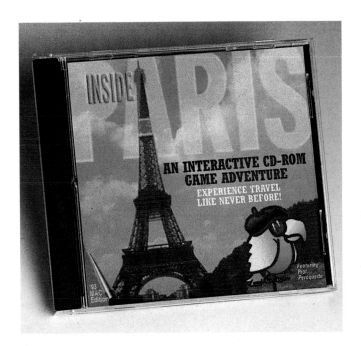

INSIDE PARIS
Company
Fox Hill Productions/Boston
Design Firm
Howie Green Design
All Design
Howie Green
Illustrator
Christopher Lowery, Howie Green

BUBBLE BOBBLE™
Company
Taito
Design Firm
Qually & Company, Inc.
Art Director
Robert Qually
Design
**Robert Qually, Karla Walusiak,
Holly Thomas, Charles Senties**
Illustrator
Ron Villani

The logo, created by airbrush on acrylic
with black line art on acetate overlay, was
developed to emphasize the overall usage
of bubbles in this game. Images appear
inside the bubbles as well, adding diversion
and difficulty.

Objective
Gamers become Bub and Bob, two hungry
brontosaurs, and battle battalions of evil
beasts by blowing and bursting billions
of bubbles.

Taito® and Bubble Bobble™ are trademarks of
Taito America Corporation. Copyright © 1988.

*THESE ARE TWO HUNGRY DINO-MIGHTS AND THEY'VE
GOT BUBBLE FIGHT'N FUN DOWN TIGHT...You and your two brontosaurus buddies, Bub
and Bob, are up to your brows in bubble trouble. You've got to battle battalions of bul-
lies by blowing and bursting billions of bubbles. It's a fast-paced bubble banquet through
100 screens of slap-happy suds. Got an appetite for fun...then get blowin'.*

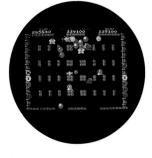

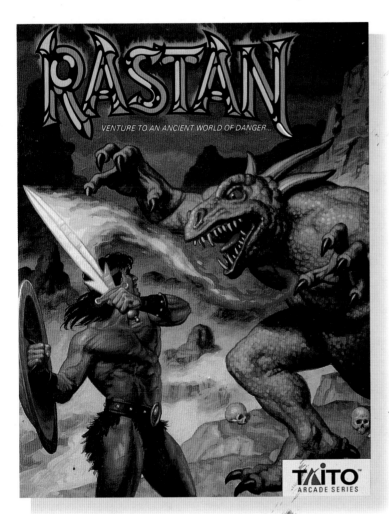

BONJOUR PROVENCE!
Company
Fox Hill Productions/Boston
Design Firm
Howie Green Design
All Design
Howie Green
Illustrator
**Christopher Lowery,
Howie Green**

RASTAN™
Company
Taito
Design Firm
Qually & Company, Inc.
Art Director
Robert Qually
Design
**Robert Qually, Karla Walusiak,
Holly Thomas, Charles Senties**
Illustrator
Tim Hildebrandt

To emphasize the importance of the sword, designers developed a typographical logo that has a "flaming, sword-like" quality, using sharp angles and edges. Colors give the appearance of light reflecting on a bi-level, shiny surface. Images were created with oil paint on canvas board. In the game, the characters travel through various caverns and caves which appear on the screen as dark blues, dark purples, and dark greens, giving these areas a gloomy setting.

Taito® and Rastan™ are trademarks of Taito America Corporation.
Copyright © 1988.

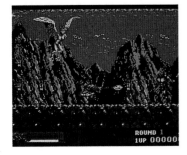  

OPERATION WOLF®

Company
Taito
Design Firm
Qually & Company, Inc.
Art Director
Robert Qually
Designer
Robert Qually, Karla Walusiak, Holly Thomas, Charles Senties
Illustrator
Don Kueker

Graphics emphasize the "military team" aspect of this game with the use of a military-like patch with insignia which appears in various sizes. The patch was created first in embroidery, in order to give the screen image a realistic, worn-in feel.

Objective
Players are members of "The Operation Wolf Team" and must rescue numerous American citizens that have been taken hostage by terrorists. The team is the only chance of survival for the hostages. Gamers must save them using commando-style tactics in a full force, armed battle.

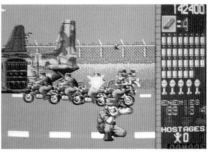

ASHES OF EMPIRE™
Company
Gametek, Inc.
Design Firm
Gametek Creative
Art Director
Stephen Curran
Designer
John Tombley
Illustrator
Glen Wexler Studio

Logo was created in Adobe Illustrator, then cast as a metal plate, photographed and retouched in Adobe Photoshop. Graphics were assembled in QuarkXPress.

Objective
In a modern world, what happens when empires fall...Inspired by the tumultuous events in Eastern Europe, **ASHES OF EMPIRE** is a complex fusion of adventure and strategy which places demands on all your powers of diplomacy and intelligence. As you enter the heartland of your adversary, you must select a tactic to bring order to chaos, while at the same time avoiding a nuclear conflict with an embittered and desperate people.

DAFFY DUCK
GAME BOY™
Company
Sunsoft
Design Firm
Moore & Price

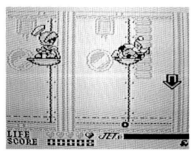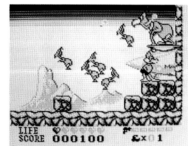

GAME BOY™
FINAL FANTASY LEGEND
Company
Nintendo of America
Design Firm
Becker Design Associates
Art Director
Rick Becker
Illustrator
Stephen Peringer

Cover airbrush illustration
with Prismacolor details.

SIMON
Company
Milton Bradley Company
Design Firm
Libby, Perszyk, Kathman
Art Director
Nan Finkenaur
Designer
Ray Perszyk, John Metz
Illustrator
Dave LaFleur
Photographer
Alan Epstein

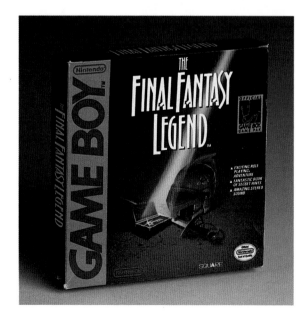

GAME BOY®
SPEEDY GONZALES
Company
Sunsoft
Design Firm
Wunderman Cato Johnson

Package is meant to look like a
hunk of cheese.

57

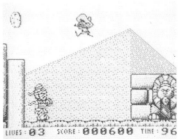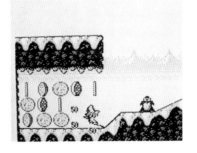

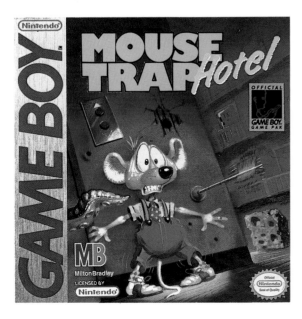

GAME BOY™
MOUSETRAP HOTEL
Company
Milton Bradley
All Design
Nan Finkenaur
Illustrator
Jim Talbot

GAME BOY™
SUPER SCRABBLE®
Company
Milton Bradley
All Design
Nan Finkenaur

Objective
The ultimate crossword game
cartridge for use with your
Nintendo GAME BOY. Compete
against a friend or against
GAME BOY to build crosswords
for the most points.

©1990 Nintendo of America Inc.

POWER GLADIATORS
Company
Milton Bradley
Art Director
Nan Finkenaur
Designer
Nan Finkenaur, David Tow

**PLAY IT BY EAR,
VOLUMES 1 AND 2**
Company
Rykodisc
Design Firm
Volume 1 -
Charles R. Brunner Design
Volume 2 -
Elissa Traher Design
Designer
Volume 1 -
Charles R. Brunner
Volume 2 -
Elissa Traher
Illustrator
Joan Campagna

A compact disc is incorporated into
the package and component design.

PLAY IT BY EAR is a board game
featuring an audio compact disc.

© 1991, 1992 Rykodisc

58

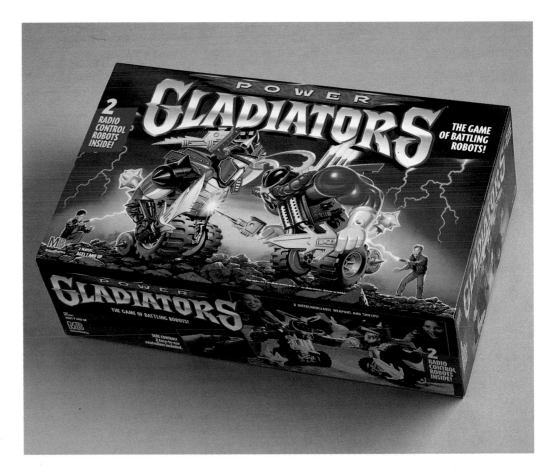

**STAR TREK: THE NEXT
GENERATION® INTERACTIVE VCR
BOARD GAME**
Company
Decipher Inc.
Art Director/Designer
Dan Burns
Illustrator
Kathleen Kripler, Dan Burns
Photographer
Bob Anders

Objective
The mission is to gain access to
five levels of the main computer by
collecting chips in your Tricorder.
Get a phaser from Security and
successfully crawl down a Jefferies
tube to attempt to win the game
by gaining control of the U.S.S.
Enterprise.

™, ® & ©1993 Paramount Pictures. All Rights Reserved.
STAR TREK is a Registered Trademark of Paramount
Pictures. Decipher Inc. Authorized User. Rules © 1993
Decipher Inc.

PARTY MANIA™
Company
Parker Brothers
Art Director
Jim Engelbrecht
Designer
Lisa Sparks
Illustrator
Jeff Stock
Photographer
Hot Shots

Objective
Make sure you go to the party
by getting rid of all your
Saturday "Chore" cards,
collecting all the "Get Ready"
tokens you need, and getting
"Mom's Stamp of Approval" so
you can be on the front porch
at 6:00 PM, ready to go.

PARTY MANIA is a trademark of Tonka Corporation for its interactive videotape board
game.

60

TALES OF THE CRYSTALS
Company
Milton Bradley
Art Director
Nan Finkenaur
Designer
**Nan Finkenaur,
Melissa Mips**
Illustrator
Don Kueker

The words begin™

pre·fix

MONOPOLY TIN®
Company
Parker Brothers
Art Director
James Engelbrecht
Illustrator
Lou Brooks

The graphics were designed to communicate the classic nature of the product. The design challenge included creating a new logotype by combining existing elements. The choice of the tin box for packaging makes the product a stand out on the shelf.

MONOPOLY and the game board design are Tonka Corporation's registered trademarks for its real estate trading game and game equipment.

PRE•FIX
Company
Merriment, Incorporated
Designer
Keith R. Evans
Photographer
Carleton Krull

The initial run was screen-printed, silver ink on box wrap.

Objective
A mix of high speed writing, super quick thinking, and clever guessing.

65

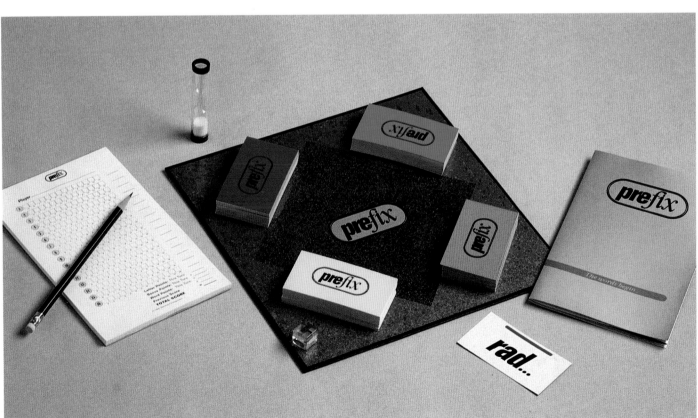

RISK®
Company
Parker Brothers
Art Director
Jim Engelbrecht
Illustrator
Steve Chorney
Photographer
Hot Shots

Cover illustrates the classic struggle that is the center of game play. A traditional illustration and computer production.

Objective
A favorite for over 30 years, this is the classic battle game of world conquest. Control entire armies and mastermind dramatic moves across the continents. Send in reinforcements...battle enemies...and conquer the world. Rules include the classic European game called Secret Mission Risk, the shorter Capital Risk game, a two-player version of standard **RISK**, plus rules variations for **RISK** experts.

Risk is Tonka Corporation's registered trademark for its world conquest game.

© 1936 PARKER BROTHERS, INC.

MONOPOLY® ANNIVERSARY
Company
Parker Brothers
Art Director
James Engelbrecht
Illustrator
Lou Brooks

Objective
This edition features a special anniversary token — the Monopoly train. There are 10 additional tokens in golden-tone finish, wooden houses and hotels, a specially designed Banker's tray and Title Deed card holder.

The package graphics and typography were designed to echo the feel of the 1930's. The new logo was used to unify the family look.

MONOPOLY and the game board design are Tonka Corporation's registered trademarks for its real estate trading game and game equipment.

68

SORRY!®
Company
Parker Brothers
Art Director
James Engelbrecht
Designer
Midnight Oil

Objective
This family classic is filled with slides, backward and forward moves, and special SORRY cards that can send you or an opponent right back to Start. It's a chase and a race, and it's never over until somebody gets all the way Home.

SORRY! is Tonka Corporation's registered trademark for its slide pursuit game.

CLASSIC GAMES

DREAM ON
Company
E & M Games
Design Firm
Monnens-Addis Design
Art Director
Steven Addis, Joanne Hom
Designer
Steven Addis
Computer
Hugh Howie

As a start-up company,
E & M Games required a
package design to command
attention among retailers and
consumers and involve its audience
too. Dream imagery icons, such as
a snake, a key, a bird, and a train,
creates a visually intriguing package.
Images drift between sleep and
consciousness, from one realm to
the other.

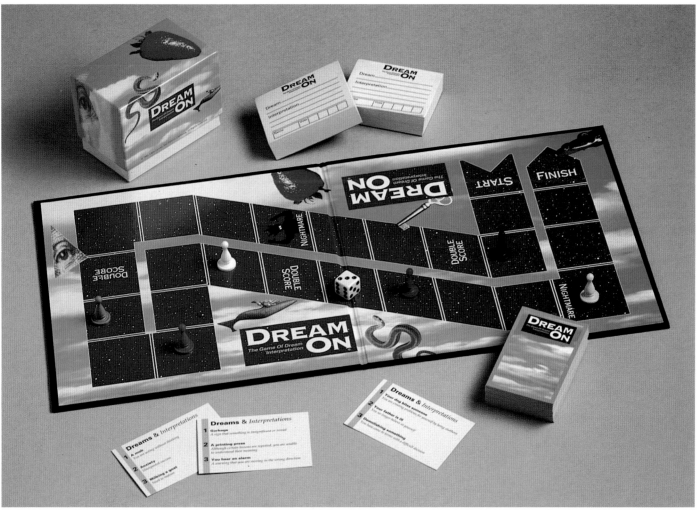

TRIBOND®
Company
Patch Products, Inc.
Design Firm
Communique Designs
Designer
David Yearick, Tim Walsh
Illustrator
Eric Lindstrom

The original package was black. It
was redesigned to add color and
a look of fun. The cover design emu-
lates the board. Graphics
created with IBM Coral Draw.

Objective
Move three game pieces along
their separate paths, and into the
respective Home spaces. Game
pieces are moved by answering **TRI-
BOND** Clue-sets. A Clue-set is
a list of three things that have a spe-
cific relationship to one another.

**TRIBOND®,
CLUE-SET CARDS #2**
Company
Patch Products, Inc.
Design Firm
Walzak Advertising & Design, Inc.
Designer
Tim Walsh, David Yearick
Illustrator
Kevin Walzak

Graphics created with Macintosh in
Adobe Illustrator.

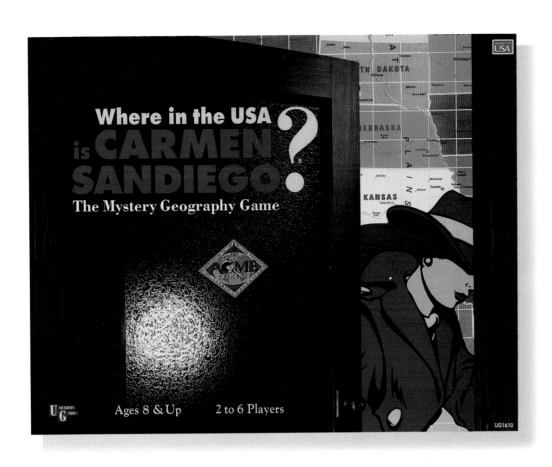

WHERE IN THE USA IS CARMEN SANDIEGO?®

Company
University Games
Design Firm
Nimbus Design
Art Director
Jeff Pinsker
Designer
Tom Finnegan
Photographer
Frank Haxton

Objective
Uncover the locations of a matching set of cards — a Warrant Card, a Loot Card, and a Crook Card — of the same color.

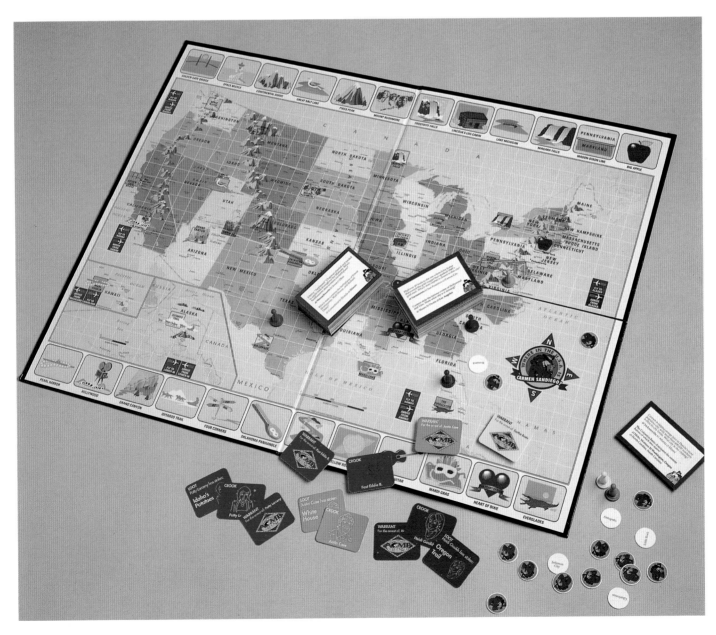

BLURT!™
Company
Patch Products, Inc.
Design Firm
Walzak Advertising & Design, Inc.
Designer
Tim Walsh
Illustrator
Kevin Walzak

Logo designed to have a fluid look. Icons on cover are from the gameboard. Graphics developed in Adobe Illustrator and Adobe Photoshop.

Objective
Be the first player to move your pawn from the Start space, clockwise along the colored path, and back to the Start space. Players or teams earn the right to move their pawn by being the first to BLURT! out a word defined by a "Defunition". A "Defunition" is a real definition to a word from *The Webster's II Riverside Children's Dictionary.*

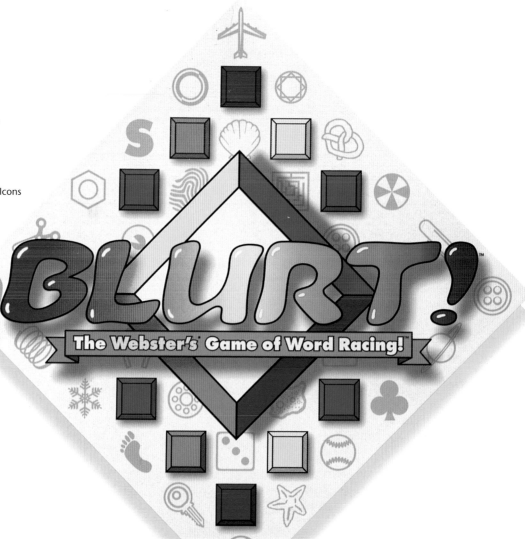

BONKERS
Company
Milton Bradley Company
Art Director
Nan Finkenaur
Designer
Nan Finkenaur
Illustrator
Richie McNeal

LIFE STORIES
Company
LifeStories, Inc.
Design Firm
Gardner Design
All Design
Nancy Gardner

Done on computer, the new package is outselling the old package 6 to 1.

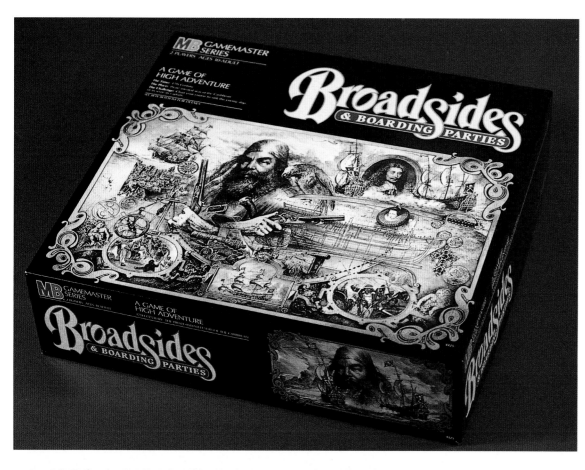

BROADSIDES
Company
Milton Bradley
All Design
Jim Bremer
Illustrator
Chet Jezerski

CLUE®
Company
Parker Brothers
Art Director
Jim Engelbrecht
Illustrator
Tim Hildebrandt

The cover illustration
portrays the sense of drama
surrounding a murder
mystery. The illustration was
combined with the computer
generated logo design.

Objective
Whodunit? Where? With What?
Was it Colonel Mustard in the
Conservatory with the Revolver?
Solve a fascinating new mystery
every time you play this classic
detective game that relies on your
sleuthing ability to deduce the
culprit, the scene of the crime, and
the murder weapon. A favorite
for generations.

CLUE is a registered trademark of Waddingtons Games
Ltd; used under license.

76

MONOPOLY®
Company
Parker Brothers
Art Director
Jim Engelbrecht
Illustrator
Lou Brooks

Photography and the new
50th Anniversary logo were
used to continue the
traditional look of the
package.

Objective
Buy! Sell! Go directly to Jail!
Buy real estate, collect rents,
build hotels - but don't go
bankrupt as you wheel and
deal in the world's most
popular, most widely played
board game.

MONOPOLY and the game board
design are Tonka Corporation's registered
trademarks for its real estate trading
game and game equipment.

78

A DAY IN THE LIFE
Company
GTE
Design Firm
**Alan Charles,
Games for Industry**
Art Director
Robert Weisberg
Designer
Alan Charles
Illustrator
Sol Korby
Photographer
Leon Kuzmanoff
Editor
Melvin J. Silverberg

CLUE®,
THE GREAT MUSEUM CAPER
Company
Parker Brothers
Design Firm
Nason/Parker Brothers
Art Director
Ted Bick
Designer
Dave Schwenderman, Ted Bick
Illustrator
Tim Hildebrandt
Photographer
Hot Shots

Objective
Who'll catch the crook who's snatching priceless paintings from the 3-D game board? The invisible thief marks down all moves in secret behind a shield...the other players work together to catch him with video cameras, motion detectors, and keen observation.

CLUE is a registered trademark and THE GREAT MUSEUM CAPER is a trademark of Waddingtons Games Ltd; used under exclusive license.

CHINESE CHESS
Company
Jackie Tan Collection
Design Firm
Jackie Tan Design Studio
All Design
Jackie Tan

Design is based on a graphic cut concept and gives an old Chinese chess set a modern look.

13 DEAD END DRIVE
Company
Milton Bradley Company
Art Director
Jim Bremer, Nan Finkenaur
Designer
**Jim Bremer, Nan Finkenaur,
David Tow**
Illustrator
Jim Talbot
Photographer
Geoff Stein

CLASSIC GAMES

TIME - THE GAME
Company
Time Magazine
Design Firm
**Alan Charles,
Games for Industry**
Art Director
Robert Weisburg
Designer
Alan Charles
Illustrator
Sol Korby
Photographer
Leon Kuzmanoff
Editor
Melvin J. Silverberg

PERPETUAL NOTION
Company
Pressman Toy Corp.
Design Firm
**Wallace & Church,
Bracchi Design**
Photographer
Wilby Studios

Lightbulb graphic is a lenticular lens
with dual graphics.

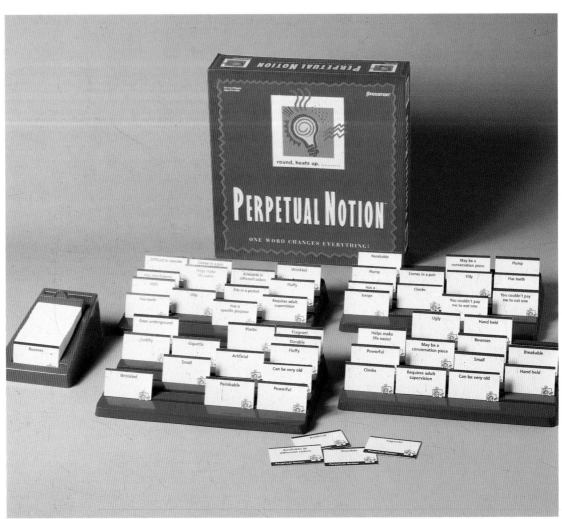

CLASSIC GAMES

SHAKIN' SORRY®
Company
Parker Brothers
Art Director
James Engelbrecht

Objective
It's the fast-playing roll 'n' grab dice game that
capitalizes on the Slide and Sorry! fun of the classic
SORRY! board game. Shake the cup full of color-coded
dice, roll 'em and join in the grab-fest as everybody
tries to be first to get 4 dice of their Home.

SORRY! is a registered trademark of Tonka Corporation for its slide
pursuit dice game.

BAFFLES
Company
Matchbox
Design Firm
Michael Standard, Inc.
Art Director
Michael Stanard
Designer
Ann Werner

CLASSIC GAMES

CARROLLTON
Company
City of Carrollton
Design Firm
Alan Charles,
Games for Industry
Art Director
Robert Weisburg
Designer
Alan Charles
Illustrator
Sol Korby
Photographer
Leon Ruzmanoff
Editor
Melvin J. Silverberg

ELEMENTO®
Company and All Design
San-Deb-Bar-Nan-Rio-Way-Corp.

Company name is the first
3 letters of the principal's
children's names.

Objective
Accumulate the most Protons
by acquiring Elements. Players
collect Protons when another
player lands on their Elements,
or when another player lands on
the Group of Elements (same color)
in which they have already acquired
one or more Elements.

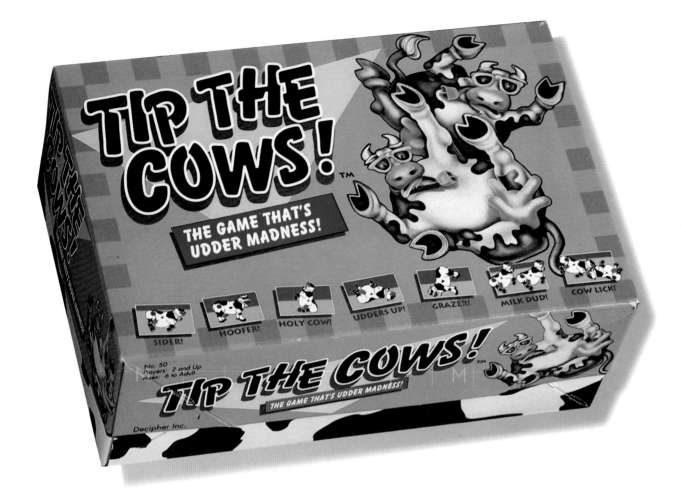

TIP THE COWS!™
Company
Decipher Inc.
Art Director
Dan Burns
Designer
Dan Burns
Illustrator
Kathleen Kridler
Photographer
Bob Ander

Objective
Tip or roll both cows (just like dice) and obtain the highest score. The point values for different cow positions are shown on the back panel of these rules.

86

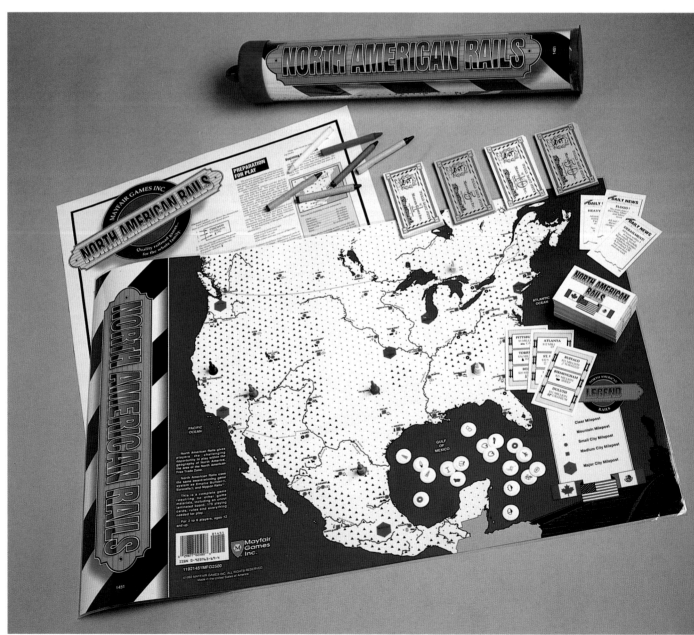

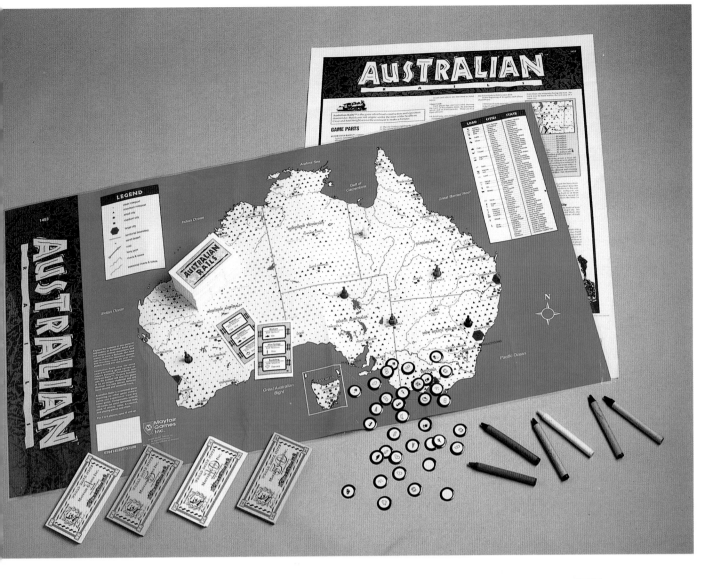

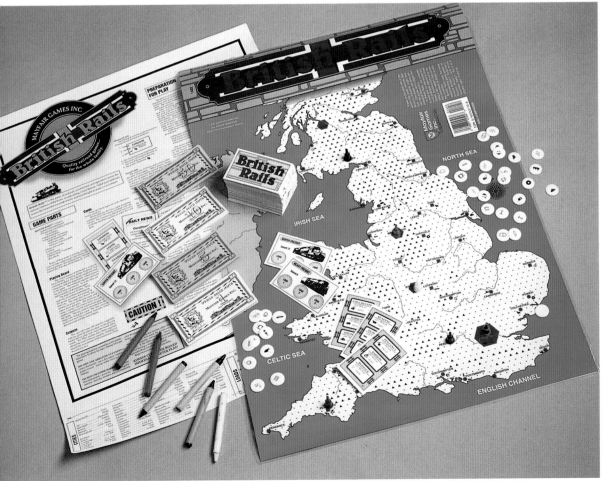

NIPPON RAILS
NORTH AMERICAN RAILS
AUSTRALIAN RAILS
BRITISH RAILS
Company
Mayfair Games, Inc.
Designer
Mike Russo
Chris Ferguson

Economical and very unique
presentation, game board
doubles as exterior packaging.
A series of train games that
take place in different locations
throughout the world.

CALIFORNIA
CLASSICS - 2.GO!
Company
Mattel
Design Firm
**Mike Salisbury
Communications, Inc.**
All Design
Mike Salisbury

A series of inexpensive
portable games

YOUR DREAMS
Company
West Games
Design Firm
**Mike Salisbury
Communications, Inc.**
Art Director/Designer
Mike Salisbury
Illustrator
Jonathan Heale

PLATTER - O' - FORTUNE
Company
West Games
Design Firm
**Mike Salisbury
Communications, Inc.**
Art Director/Designer
Mike Salisbury
Illustrator
John Van Hamersvele

HEADLINE DEADLINE
Company
Family Games, Inc.
Design Firm
Family Games
Art Director/Designer
Susan Hebblethwaite
Computer Graphic
Johanne Leduc

Objective
The object of the game is
to guess the 4 missing facts
from a news headline before
advancing towards the finish
line with the help of a
special die, a quick mind,
and fast hands.

**INTERFERENCE
/NINCOMPOOP**
Company
Family Games, Inc.
Design Firm
Family Games
Art Director/Designer
Susan Hebblethwaite
Computer Graphic
Johanne Leduc

Product designed so both
games use all the same
game components.

Objective
The object of the game is to
either cause interference or
avoid interfering with other
players as you race your
pawns to the Finish.

Objective
The object of the game is to
be the first NINCOMPOOP
to reach 100 points by
performing a number of
zany stunts.

CLASSIC GAMES

ARCH RIVAL®
Company
Parker Brothers
Design Firm
Primo Angeli Inc.
Art Director
**Carlo Pagoda, Primo Angeli,
Steven Strumpf**
Designer
Darryl Reed, Carlo Pagoda
Illustrator
Darryl Reed, Kelly Burke

Advertised as a game of "reckless
abandon, balance, nerves, and
suspense." The package needed to
communicate visually to consumers
what the concept was all about.
The kinetic graphic design vividly
conveys both the appearance —
the "arch"— and the dynamics of
the game.

PASS THE PIGS™
Company
Milton Bradley Company
Art Director/Designer
Nan Finkenaur
Illustrator
Thomas Blackshear

Objective
The hilarious game of chance that
uses pigs as dice! Toss those pigs
and see how they fall: you could win
big…or you could lose all! If the
piggies land on their back or feet,
rack up points to turn up the heat.
You'll have even more to shout
about if those pigs come to land on
their jowls or snout. But if the two
porkers even touch: gone are your
points…thanks very much.

The Go Hog-Wild Dice Game

PASS THE PIGS

SCATTERGORIES®
Company
Milton Bradley
Design Firm
Sibley Peteet Design
Art Director
Don Sibley, Jim Bremer
Designer/Illustrator
John Evans

Objective
How many categories you can match using words that start with the same letter. You rolled an "R": A U.S. city...Rochester! Can you complete your list before time runs out? Only answers that are different from everybody else's get points; the highest scorer in 3 rounds ends up the winner.

CELEBRITY TABOO®
Company
Milton Bradley
Design Firm
Sibley Peteet Design
Art Director
Don Sibley, Jim Bremer
Designer/Illustrator
John Evans

Objective
Have unspeakable fun guessing famous personalities. Get your team to say *Michelangelo* without using the clues *sculptor*, *marble*, *Pieta*, *David*, or *Sistine Chapel*. Or how about describing *Dracula* without using *Vampire*, *Transylvania*, *bloodsucker*, *coffin*, or *neck*? Plays just like the original favorite, **TABOO**, and features 1,008 celebrities to challenge and entertain you.

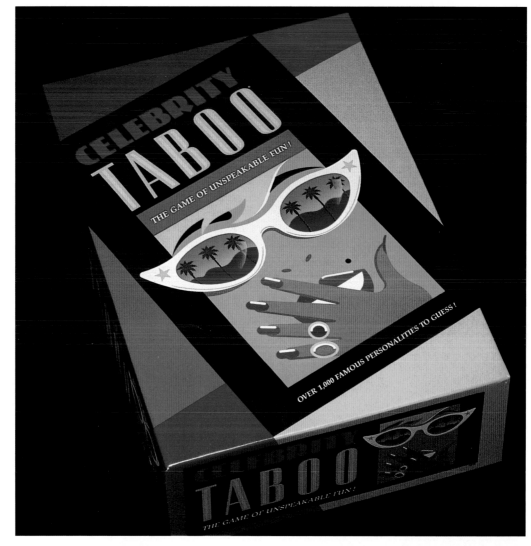

TABOO™
Company
Milton Bradley
Design Firm
Sibley Peteet Design
Art Director
Jim Bremer, Don Sibley
Designer/Illustrator
Don Sibley

Objective
Give word clues to your teammates without using any of the expressions that are taboo. Players on the opposite team keep you honest by "buzzing" if you use one of the taboo words as a clue. The object is to complete as many word cards as you can in 60 seconds.

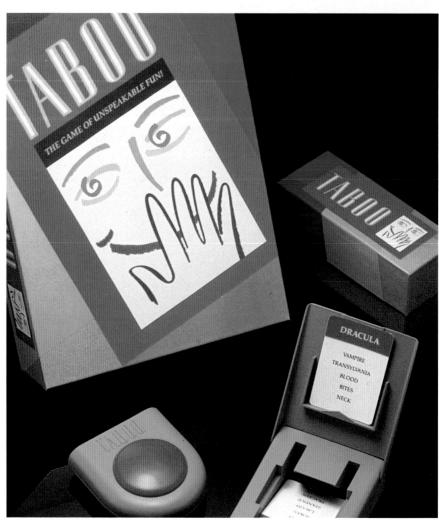

GUESSTURES™
Company
Milton Bradley
Design Firm
Sibley Peteet Design
Art Director
Don Sibley, Jim Bremer
Designer/Illustrator
David Beck

Objective
Snap the Mimer-Timer shut to start the clock and let all the fun-filled theatrics begin. Get your teammates to guess which words are showing on the cards in the Mimer-Timer... but quickly, before the cards drop out of sight. The words get more difficult as you go along.

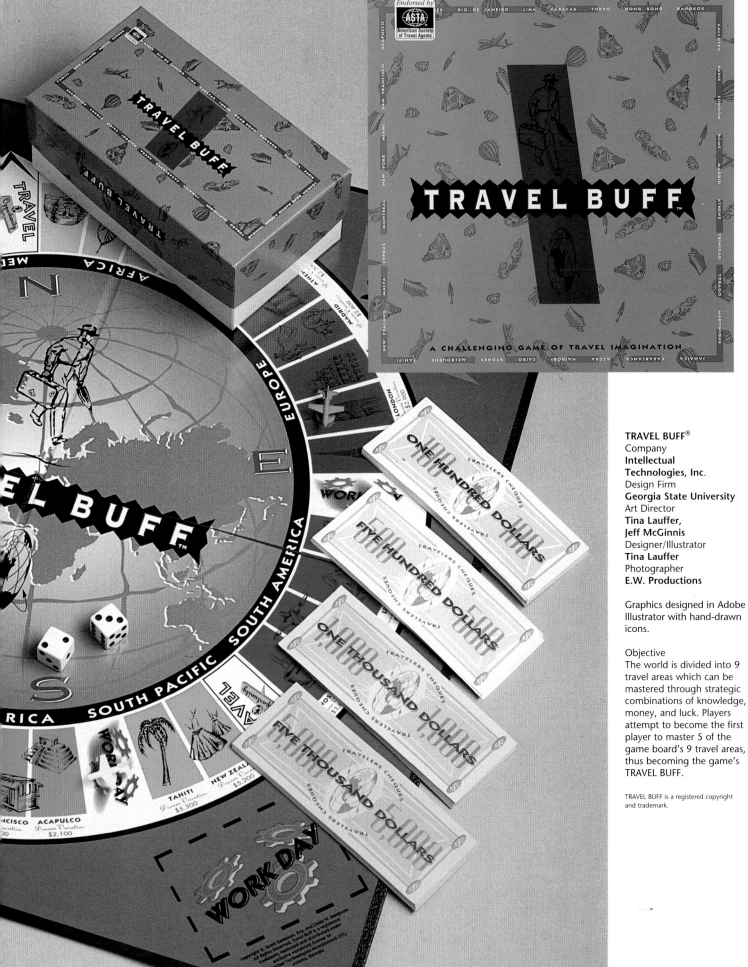

TRAVEL BUFF®
Company
**Intellectual
Technologies, Inc.**
Design Firm
Georgia State University
Art Director
**Tina Lauffer,
Jeff McGinnis**
Designer/Illustrator
Tina Lauffer
Photographer
E.W. Productions

Graphics designed in Adobe
Illustrator with hand-drawn
icons.

Objective
The world is divided into 9
travel areas which can be
mastered through strategic
combinations of knowledge,
money, and luck. Players
attempt to become the first
player to master 5 of the
game board's 9 travel areas,
thus becoming the game's
TRAVEL BUFF.

TRAVEL BUFF is a registered copyright
and trademark.

ADULT GAMES

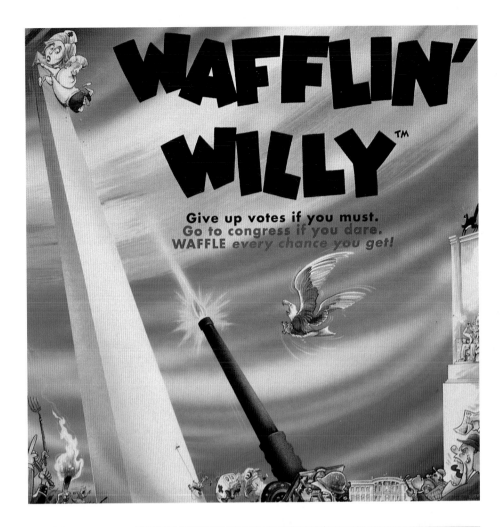

WAFFLIN' WILLY™
Company
Right Angle, Inc.
Design Firm
Right Angle, Inc.
Art Director
Kevin Russell
Designer/Illustrator
Mark Martin

Objective
The object of **WAFFLIN' WILLY** is to run through your presidency hanging on to as many votes as you can while trying not to let your past catch up with you. Like the real thing, you begin in the middle and continuously move left. The Wafflin' Willy who reaches the end with the most votes wins the game!

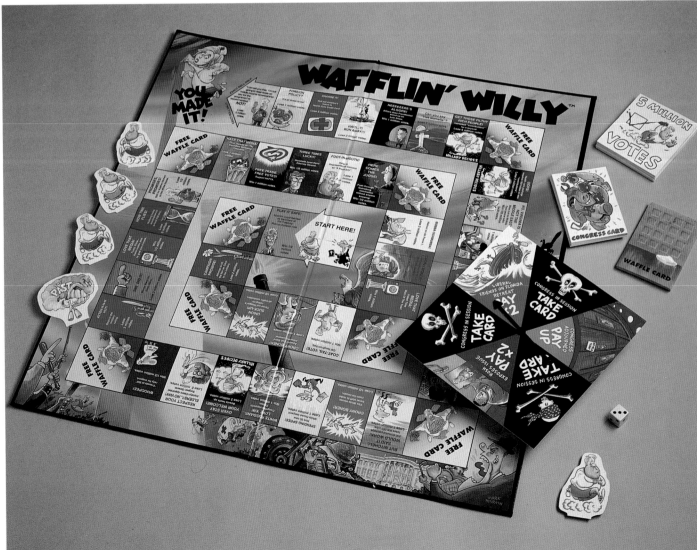

BOTTLE TOPPS®
Company
Parker Brothers
Art Director
Jim Engelbrecht
Photographer
Hot Shots

Objective
Put your balancing skill to the ultimate test as you stack 'em high and stack 'em wide. Decide how high then take turns stacking the real wood chips. When you reach the agreed-upon number of levels, cap off the stack with the red "Stopper" top.

BOTTLE TOPPS is a registered trademark of Alsip & Co. Licensed by © Alsip & Co. U.S. Patent Pending.

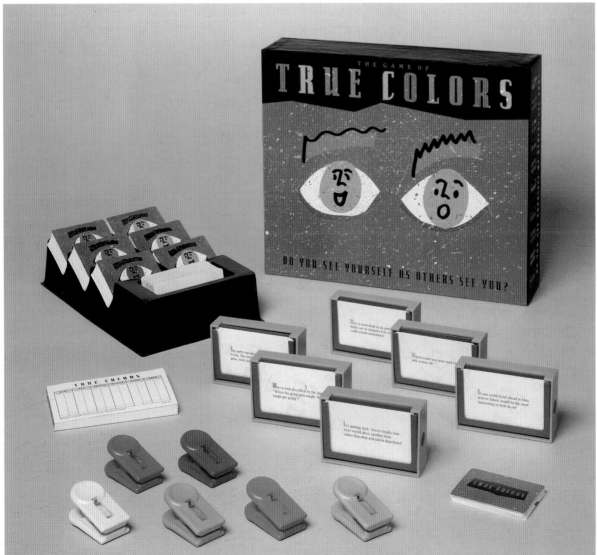

TRUE COLORS™
Company
Milton Bradley
Design Firm
Sibley Peteet Design
Art Director
Nan Finkenaur
Designer/Illustrator
Diana McKnight
Photographer
Geoff Stein

Objective
Once everyone has cast their ballots, try to predict whether you received the most, some, or no votes. Make the most correct predictions to win.

ADULT GAMES

LIFE OF THE PARTY –
PASSION CABANA IN HAVANA™
ROCKIN' LATE AT THE PROM OF '58™
THE COFFEE HOUSE MURDER™
WHO KILLED ROGER ELLINGTON™

Company
Milton Bradley
Design Firm
Sibley Peteet Design
Art Director
Jim Bremer, Don Sibley
Designer/Illustrator
Don Sibley

ONE BY ONE
Company
Gilbert Paper
Design Firm
Sayles Graphic Design
All Design
John Sayles

Only one color was used to produce the game and
promotion materials.

WORD BY WORD
Company
Word Origin, Inc.
Design Firm
**The Design Office of
Wong & Yeo**
Art Director
Valerie Wong
Designer
Valerie Wong
Photographer
**Troy Wood, Peggy Day,
North Light**

SECRETS
Company
Milton Bradley Company
Design Firm
Tim Girvin Design
Art Director
Nan Finkenaur
Designer
Tim Girvin, Anton Kimball

LES VINS DE FRANCE™
Company
The Brandywine Game Co.
Design Firm
Bb Design, Inc.
Designer
Brenda Best-Howland
Illustrator
Cynthia McGrellis
Photographer
Frederick Mullison

Objective
Players take a gourmet tour of France
visiting the quality wine-making regions,
and acquiring cards representing over 90
years of wine. It all adds up to a fun-filled
way for 2 to 6 people to spend 1 to 2 hours
at a game board, while increasing their
knowledge and appreciation of French
wines and cuisine!

CASINO ROYALE
Company
The Learning Experience, Inc.
Art Director
Suzanne Proffer
Designer
A.P. Dubarry, Jr.

Objective
To win by having the most net worth at the end of a predetermined period of play. Net worth is determined by adding up each player's chips and casinos.

© A.P. Dubarry, Jr. 1992

DON'T WAKE DADDY®
Company
Parker Brothers
Art Director
Steven Stumpf
Illustrator
Kim Passey

Objective
You race to the fridge for a midnight snack, match colors, recognize numbers, and keep pushing the button on Daddy's alarm clock: Will you be the one who wakes Daddy — and makes him sit straight up in bed?

DON'T WAKE DADDY is a registered trademark of Tonka Corporation for its alarm clock midnight snack game and game equipment.

102

DON'T PANIC®
Company
Milton Bradley
Design Firm
Sibley Peteet Design
Art Director
Don Sibley, Jim Bremer
Designer
Dianna McKnight
Illustrator
Gary Basemann

Objective
The name-a-lot-on-the-spot game. Start out by naming 3 examples each turn for all the categories listed on your card. Then try to name 4 examples each turn...all before time runs out.

©1990 David Mair.

JACK SPRAT COULD
EAT NO FAT
HIS WIFE COULD
EAT NO LEAN
AND SO BETWEEN
THE TWO OF THEM
THEY LICKED
THE PLATTER CLEAN

AN EDUCATIONAL GAME TO HELP YOU EXPLORE THE FOOD GUIDE PYRAMID WHILE LEARNING TO BUDGET YOUR "FAT BUCKS."

JACK SPRATS TABLE
Company
Kansas Lean
All Design
Gardner + Greteman

This educational game teaches children the value of nutrition in a fun, progressive way.

Objective
The first player who acquires food cards representing the minimum number of servings of each food group in the Food Guide Pyramid, and who has at least one "fat buck" left, wins **JACK SPRATS TABLE**.

105

UNCLE WIGGILY™
Company
Milton Bradley
Art Director/Designer
Nan Finkenaur
Illustrator
Tim Hildebrant

Objective
Uncle Wiggily invites youngsters to join him on a walk down the forest path. Along the way, kids meet Uncle Wiggily's pals and try to avoid bumping into nasty critters like the Sneaky Skeezicks or the Scillery Scallery Alligator. Players draw cards and follow the simple rhymes to move, match numbers and symbols. First boy or girl to arrive at Dr. Possum's house wins!

©1989 M.R. Garis.

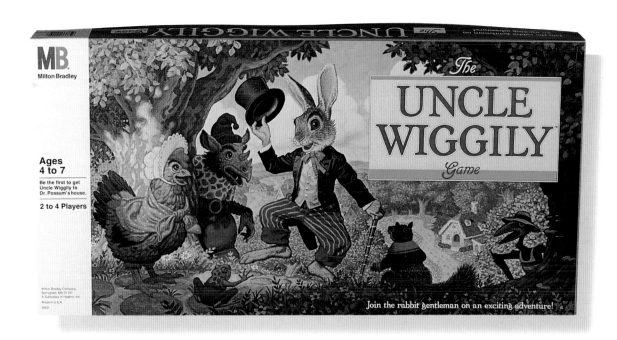

BACK OFF! BUZZARD™
Company
Milton Bradley
Art Director
Jim Bremer
Designer
Jim Bremer, Erik Ela
Illustrator
Lon Busch

Objective
The motorized escape game where players vie for who will be first to guide their two explorers across the ancient ruins and back to camp.

ASK ZANDAR
Company
Milton Bradley
Art Director
Nan Finkenaur
Designer
**Nan Finkenaur,
David Toru**
Illustrator
Bill Mather
Photographer
Geoff Stein
Logo
Carmine Vecchio

**CHILDREN'S
GAMES**

BEAKMAN'S WORLD
Company
Pressman Toy Corp.
Design Firm
Bracchi Design
Photographer
Wilby Studios

Objective
Be the first player to collect 7 beakers from the lab. Take a breather when you land on a Beakmania! space and answer one of the over 300 questions in the game. You also get a beaker any time you are able to perform one of the five great Beakman Challenges: Rocket Action, Lever Launch, Magnet Move, InertiaStack Attack and Domin-uh-oh! Based on the popular television show that has turned learning into excitement and fun, this game features the most popular parts of the acclaimed **BEAKMAN'S WORLD**.

BOGGLE® JR. NUMBERS
Company
Parker Brothers
Art Director
James Engelbrecht
Illustrator
Illustrated Alaskan Moose
Photographer
Hot Shots

Graphics computer designed using Macintosh System. Design and photography create an inviting educational look.

Objective
"1...2...3..." These 10 fun-filled numbers games use colorful picture/number cards and 8 number cubes to help preschoolers recognize numbers, count, do simple addition, and learn about money. The built-in timer adds to the challenge and the fun — and different levels of play let the game grow with the child.

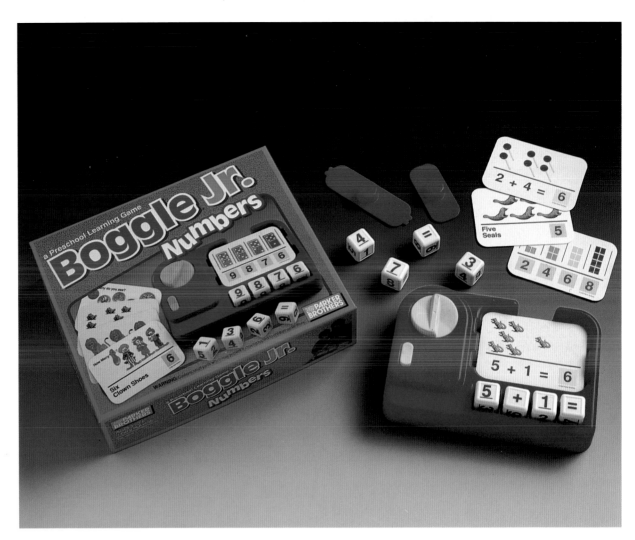

BOGGLE® JR. LETTERS
Company
Parker Brothers
Art Director
James Engelbrecht
Illustrator
Illustrated Alaskan Moose
Photographer
Hot Shots

Objective
"A...B...C" It's the original Boggle Jr. game. with picture/word cards and letter cubes. The different levels of play in these fun-filled matching and spelling games adjust to a child's own level, so they grow with the child as they help him or her learn important letter and word recognition skills.

BOGGLE is Tonka Corporation's registered trademark for its picture card and letter cube spelling game and game equipment. Rules ©1988, 1992 Parker Brothers, Division of Tonka Corporation, Beverly, MA 01915.

CHILDREN'S GAMES

SPLAT!™
Company
Milton Bradley Company
Art Director /Designer
Nan Finkenaur
Illustrator
Jim Talbot
Photographer
Geoff Stein
Logo
Jeffrey Spear

Objective
It's a madcap charge to the finish. Who'll survive, who'll be squished flat?

109

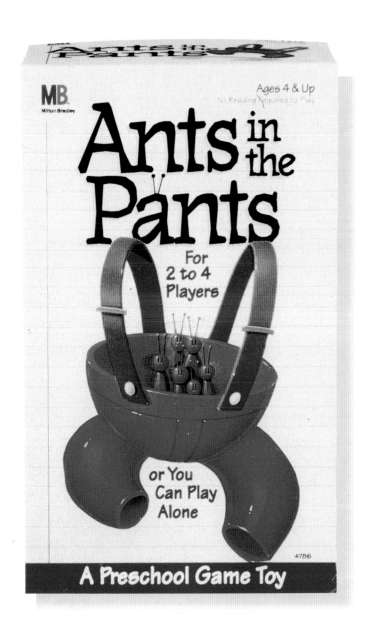

ANTS IN THE PANTS®
Company
Milton Bradley
Design Firm
Milton Bradley Graphic Arts
Art Director/Designer
Debbie Walsh

SHARK ATTACK ® BOWLING
Company
Milton Bradley
Art Director/Designer
Jim Bremer
Illustrator
Steam

Objective
This nasty mechanical shark is looking to bowl over a school of
frightened fish. Just wind him up, aim, and watch as he takes off,
slowly at first, then with a pouncing surge! Knock over the most
fish pins to win.

KIDS GAMES™ -
LITTLE RED RIDING HOOD,
GOLDILOCKS AND THE THREE BEARS,
THREE LITTLE PIGS
Company
Decipher Inc.
Art Director/Designer
Dan Burns
Illustrator
Kathleen Kridler, Dan Burns
Photographer
Bob Ander

Objective
Children's best-loved storybooks come to life in this delightful
series of beginner's games for kids. Designed by an expert to
stimulate and entertain the youngest players, these games are
fun, easy to play and beautifully packaged. Simply spin and
move along the brightly colored spaces to collect objects and
win the game!

CHILDREN'S
GAMES

FLYING THUNDER
Company
Milton Bradley
Art Director
Jim Bremer
Designer
Jim Bremer, Erik Ela
Illustrator
Mark Riedy

114

DENNIS THE MENACE™
Company
Pressman Toy Corp.
Design Firm
Bracchi Design
Photographer
Wilby Studios

Objective
Switchblade Sam has
stolen good ol' Mr.
Wilson's coin collection
and you have to capture
him. You'll need some
rope (at Joey's house),
some tape (in the
treehouse), and your
wagon (in your
backyard) to get
Switchblade Sam. There's
Margaret. She wants to kiss
you, so you'd better stay away
from her or you'll lose a turn! And
whatever you do, don't step on
Mr. Wilson's prize orchid. He'll
get plenty mad and you'll lose a turn
too.

© Warner Bros. Dennis The Menace is a trademark of Hank

SCATTERGORIES® JUNIOR
Company
Milton Bradley
Design Firm
Sibley Peteet Design
Art Director
Don Sibley, Jim Bremer
Designer/Illustrator
John Evans

Objective
Roll the big letter die and see if you can find answers starting with the same letter to categories such as: Girl's Names, Things You Do in the Summer, Desserts or Candy, Things at a Circus, etc. Each list has 6 categories to be completed before time runs out. Seventy-two different categories in all.

FUTURE STORIES
Company
Life Stories
Design Firm
Gardner Design
Art Director/Designer
Nancy Gardner

HIDDEN TALENTS™
Company
Pressman Toy Corp.
Design Firm
Bracchi Design
Photographer
Wilby Studios

Objective
It's the best way to learn the wackiest and tackiest things about
your friends! Hidden Talents is the perfect game for fun-loving
"tween" girls! To start, read aloud from one of the 180 question
cards. It may ask: "Which player owns the most hats?" or "Which
player will do the best imitation of a high-fashion model?" or
"Which player will list the most toppings for an ice cream sundae?"
Place your secret vote for the player you think will come out on
top. After 10 rounds, the player who has the most points wins!

WILLIE GO BOOM™
Company
Parker Brothers
Design Firm
Illustrated Alaskan Moose
Art Director/Designer
Karen Schmidt
Illustrator
Mark Tracey
Photographer
Geoff Stein

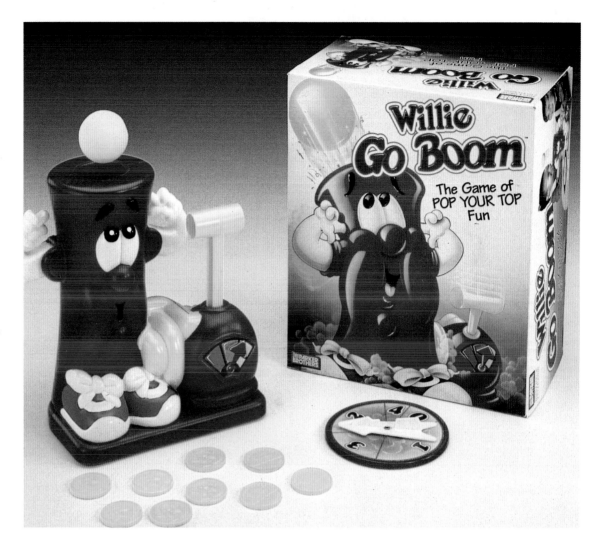

SHAMU™
PROTECT OUR SEAS™ GAME
Company
Pressman Toy Corp.
Design Firm
Bracchi Design
Photographer
Wilby Studios

Objective
In this colorful and exciting 3-D
game players have a fun way to
learn about the environment. Move
your Shamu character around the
sea. To win, you must be the first
player to save 2 of Shamu's friends
from the hazards. Rescue Dolly the
Dolphin from the net, Penny and
Pete Penguin from the iceberg, O.P.
Otter from an oil slick and Baby
Shamu from being beached. Get
them to safety on the Funship then
get your Shamu back to join them.

**CHILDREN'S
GAMES**

BRAIN QUEST™
Company
University Games
Design Firm
Draper & Liew
Art Director
Jeff Pinsker
Designer
Kwang Liew

Objective
Be the first player to reach the Finish; players race along the path by correctly answering questions. The Peek & See Cards are designed so that readers can play along too.

GET AHEAD GAMES
Company
Pressman Toy Corp.
Design Firm
Bracchi Design
Photographer
Wilby Studios

'SMATH®
Objective
The game that makes math fun!
Features crossword-puzzle type game
play with bonus point squares! Two
levels of play make **'SMATH** a fun
learning game that is as simple or
complex as players want!

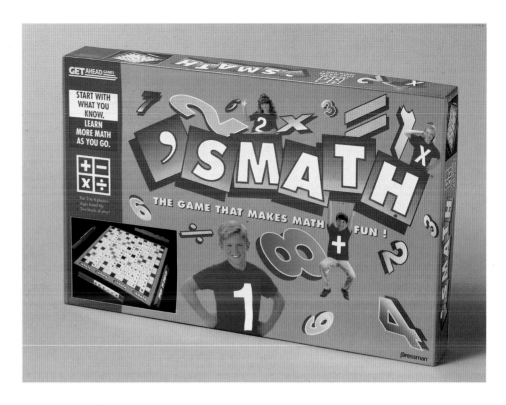

SPELLWAY™
Objective
The game that makes spelling
F-U-N! Sharpen your spelling skills in
an exciting race-to-the-finish game!
Make words with your letter cards and
move ahead. The more letters you use,
the faster you'll get there! Correctly
spell words from the Speller Pack and
you'll really leap ahead! Two levels of
difficulty let beginners and advanced
spellers play at the same time. Be the
first to reach the castle and you'll be
crowned the best speller in all the land!

Spellway is a trademark of Transatlantic Marketing Co.

STATE THE FACTS™
Objective
Take a tour across the United States
and learn fascinating facts about
geography, history, ecology,
entertainment, and more! From coast
to coast, players will learn all kinds of
interesting things about the United
States in a fun, exciting way! The
journey begins when players "take off"
from different airports and land in a
region of the country. Answer
questions correctly and earn a souvenir
from that region. The first player to
collect a souvenir card from each
region wins!

**CHILDREN'S
GAMES**

**LOONEY TUNES
SMUSH 'EM™**
Company
Tyco
Design Firm
Scrambled Eggz Productions
Art Director
Lauren Smith
Designer
Jim Mendillo
Illustrator
Eddie Young
Photographer
Mark Homan Photography

Objective
To be the first to reach the Finish.
That's all folks!

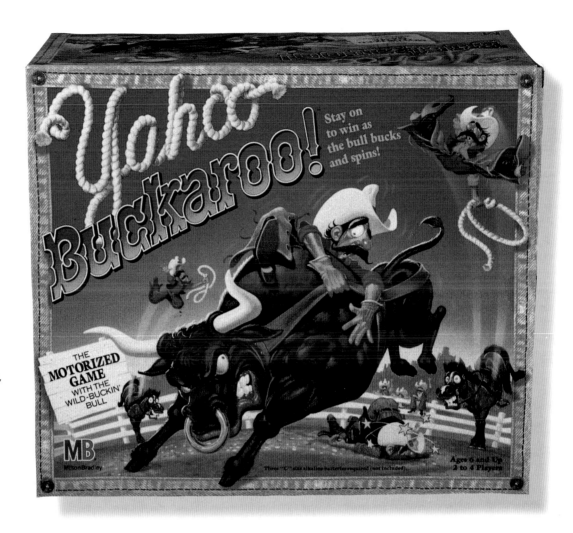

YAHOO BUCKAROO!™
Company
Milton Bradley Company
Art Director
Nan Finkenaur
Designer
Nan Finkenaur
Illustrator
Jim Talbot
Photographer
Geoff Stein
Logo
Bill Watkins

Objective
Find out if you can stay atop the spinning, bucking motorized bull. Just place a cowboy on your horse, aim, and send your man flying through the air. End up with the most cowboys hanging on to the bull once it comes to a stop and you're the winner.

122

SAVED BY THE BELL™
Company
Pressman Toy Corp.
Design Firm
Bracchi Design
Photographer
Wilby Studios

Objective
Spend an outrageous day at Bayside High with NBC-TV's Saved By The Bell gang! The most popular "Tweens" TV show on the air today!

20 QUESTIONS® NATURE AND SCIENCE

Company
University Games
Design Firm
The Mednick Group
Art Director
Bob Moog
Designer
Dan Simon
Illustrator
John Smeaton

Objective
Correctly identify well-known topics from the world of nature and science through a series of clues. The first player to reach the Finish wins the game.

MONOPOLY® JUNIOR
Company
Parker Brothers
Art Director
Jim Engelbrecht
Illustrator
Jeff Stock

Traditional illustration to convey
MONOPOLY to younger game
players.

Objective
Fast-paced junior version of the
world's most popular game. Set
up ticket booths on Boardwalk
amusements and collect fees while
Chance cards send you around
the colorful carnival board. You'll
add, subtract, and multiply the
money you collect.

MONOPOLY is a registered trademark of Tonka
Corporation for its real estate trading game and
game equipment.

CLUE® - LITTLE DETECTIVE™
Company
Parker Brothers
Art Director/Designer
Ted Bick
Illustrator
Alastair Graham
Photographer
Hot Shots

British Illustrator Alastair Graham
was the perfect choice to capture
the flavor of a Victorian Mansion
and to help solve the logistics of
making the board work.

Objective
Scared by a bump in the Boddy
Mansion attic, the Little Detectives
race to the front gate by matching
color dots along the track filled with
secret passages, "BOO!" cards and
lots of other spooky things.

CLUE is a registered trademark of Waddingtons
Games Ltd; used under license.

**CHILDREN'S
GAMES**

WIPEOUT
Company
Mattel
Design Firm
Mike Salisbury
Communications
Art Director
Jim Wolfe
Designer
Mike Salisbury
Illustrator
Greg Huber, Bruce Wolf
Photographer
Andrew Neuhard

BEVERLY HILLS, 90210™
Company
Milton Bradley
Art Director/Designer
Sera Chilson

Objective
Find out how much you know about teens from all over the country. Guess how 1600 high school kids responded to 384 revealing questions. Make the most correct guesses to reach the end of the gamepath first, and you're the winner.

CHILDREN'S
GAMES

PIE FACE™
Company
Parker Brothers
Art Director
Jim Engelbrecht
Designer
Lisa Sparks
Illustrator
Tommy Stubbs

Used traditional illustration techniques combined with computer production to create a special 3D game board.

Objective
Billy Blueberry, Annie Apple, Jerry Cherry and Peach Melba are having a pie-eating contest and you get to feed them. If you pick the right flavor piece, slide it in. If somebody else reveals your flavor, use your memory skills to remember where you saw it so you can pick it next turn. (Watch out for the Dirty Sock.)

PIE FACE is a trademark of Tonka Corporation for its pie-eating memory skills game.

PEANUT BUTTER & JELLY™
Company
Parker Brothers
Art Director
Jim Engelbrecht
Designer
Lisa Sparks
Illustrator
Mitch Hyatt

Traditional illustration and computer production.

Objective
Race to see who'll be first to make a peanut butter and jelly sandwich by matching all the necessary ingredients. Spin up a piece of bread, then spin peanut butter and jelly, and finally top off each with another piece of bread.

Peanut Butter & Jelly is a trademark of Tonka Corporation for its sandwich-making game.

CHILDREN'S GAMES

ALPHABET SOUP®

Company
Parker Brothers
Art Director
Steven Strumpf
Illustrator
American Artist

Objective
This alphabet soup has all the ingredients — from Apple to Zipper. In "Soup's On", the silly chef has mixed up all the letters in his soup. Youngsters must put them back in alphabetical order by matching them to the letter and picture on the edge of the bowl. Includes game play variation, "Second Helping."

ALPHABET SOUP is a registered trademark of Tonka Corporation for its letter-matching board game.

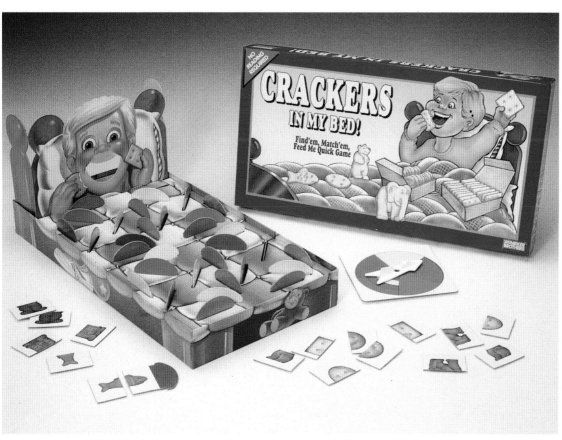

CRACKERS IN MY BED®

Company
Parker Brothers
Art Director
Steven Strumpf
Illustrator
American Artist

Objective
Players find and match cracker-half cards hidden in the boy's quilt, then pop the matched cracker into his wide-open grin. Reinforces color and shape recognition and memory skills.

CRACKERS IN MY BED is a registered trademark of Tonka Corporation for its memory and cracker-matching dimensional game equipment.

CHILDREN'S GAMES

DONUT DISASTER™
Company
Parker Brothers
Art Director
Steve Krupsky
Illustrator
Mitch Hyatt

Graphics were produced traditionally. Logo created in Adobe Illustrator.

Objective
Be first to pile up all the color donuts on the wacky donut machine before it explodes and sends everybody's donuts flying. When will it blow? You never know.

DONUT DISASTER is a trademark of Tonka Corporation for its ditsy donut machine game and game equipment. U.S. Patent Pending.

128

TRIVIAL PURSUIT® JUNIOR
Company
Parker Brothers
Art Director/Designer
Karen Schmidt
Illustrator
Jack Graham
Photographer
Geoff Stein

3-D clay sculptures were created and photographed. Mechanicals were created in Adobe Illustrator 5.0. Game board was a gigabyte file.

Objective
This special kids' edition uses a fun format similar to the adults', with specially written questions and answers for kids in these subjects: Every Day, Fun, Science, Stories & Songs, Nature, and Games. Features an exciting new look and updated questions.

The Trademark TRIVIAL PURSUIT® and the distinctive design of the game board, game cards, and related proprietary rights are registered trademarks of Horn Abbot Ltd. for the games distributed and sold in the U.S. under exclusive license to Parker Brothers. Division of Tonka Corporation.

CHILDREN'S GAMES

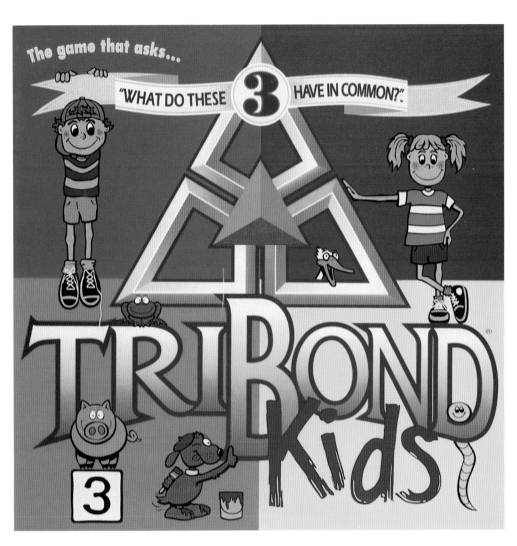

TRIBOND® KIDS
Company
Patch Products, Inc.
Design Firm
Walzak Advertising & Design, Inc.
Designer
Tim Walsh, David Yearick
Illustrator
Kevin Walzak

Graphics developed in
Adobe Illustrator.

Objective
Be the first player or team
to move your game piece from
The Purple Triangle, clockwise
around the board and back into
The Purple Triangle. Game pieces
are moved by answering TRIBOND
KIDS Clue-sets. A Clue-set is a list
of three things that has something
in common.

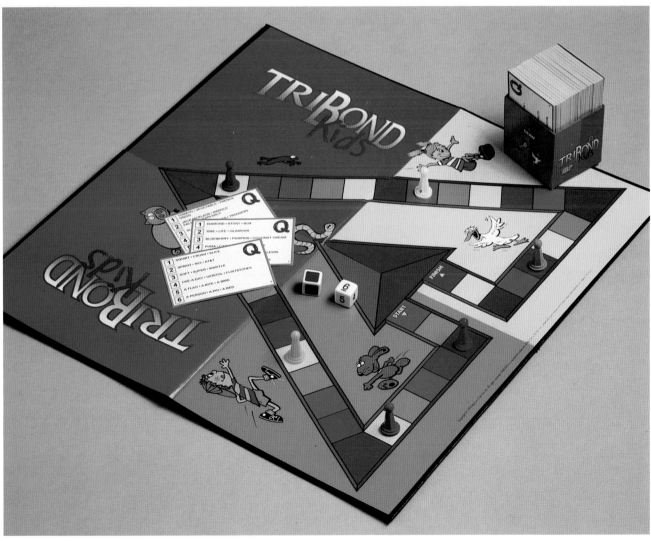

DON'T GET RATTLED!™
Company
Milton Bradley
Art Director
Jim Bremer
Designer
Jim Bremer, John Nelson
Illustrator
Jim Talbot

U.S. Patent Pending

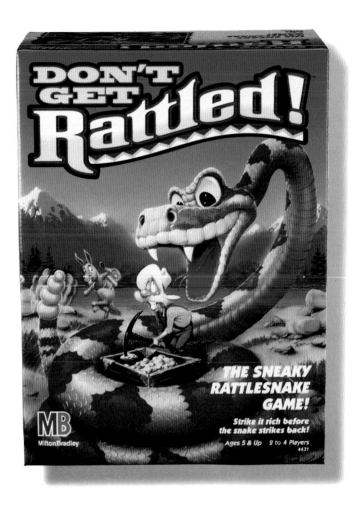

SNARDVARK™
Company Firm
Parker Brothers
Art Director/Designer
Karen Schmidt
Illustrator
Mark Tracey
Photographer
Geoff Stein

Objective
The hungry Snardvark is gobbling up snard snacks - can you out-run his tongue? When his spinning eyes stop on your color, move your Snard along the retractable-tongue track. Reach the tip before he pops you into his mouth, and you win. 'Cause if you don't, you're lunch!

SNARDVARK is a trademark of Tonka Corporation for its snard-gobbling game and game equipment. U.S. Patent No. 4,257,610.

PERFECTION®
Company
Milton Bradley
Art Director
Jim Bremer, Erik Ela
Designer
Jim Bremer

Objective
Race the clock and see if you can match all the shapes before the tray pops up. There are 25 different shapes to be placed into the correct holes on the game tray. Winner is the player who matches all the shapes in the least amount of time.

BLAST OUT™
Company
Parker Brothers
Design Firm
Javier Romero Design Inc.
Art Director
Ted Bick

A number of design approaches were tried. The final design was a simple computer execution.

Objective
Gather your opponents. Take your positions. Load your shooters. Catapult your balls into the amazing blast of air and watch them battle for position.

BLAST OUT is a trademark of Tonka Corporation for its air-power, air-stream skill and action game and game equipment. U.S. Patent Pending.

MB
Milton Bradley
You're the Croc Doc in this game of daffy dentistry!
Crocodile
DENTIST™
Ages 4 and Up
Pull the croc's teeth without getting chomped!
2 to 4 Players
Caution: Small parts may be hazardous to children under 3 years of age.
Milton Bradley Company
Springfield, MA 01101
A Subsidiary of Hasbro, Inc.
Made in U.S.A.
4153

CROCODILE DENTIST™
Company
Milton Bradley
Art Director/Designer
Sera Chilson
Illustrator
Mary Grace Eubanks

Objective
Just open the croc's jaw and, each
turn, try to pull out one of his teeth
with the special tooth extractor.
Before long, one poor player hits a
nerve when the croc shuts his
mouth with a growl and lunges
forward and that player is out of the
game. Winner is the last surviving
CROCODILE DENTIST.

SPIDER ATTACK™

Company
Parker Brothers
Art Director/Designer
Karen Schmidt
Illustrator
Roger Huyssen
Photographer
Geoff Stein

Package graphics is an air brush illustration. The rules art and mechanical were created in Adobe Illustrator.

Objective
Lots of suspense, because you never know when this dangling spider is going to swoop and attack! He hangs by a thread and drops toward you, inch by inch. He plunges and lifts you up with his sticky fly-catcher feet. The only way to safety is to get all your Flies off the web — before you're snagged.

SPIDER ATTACK is a trademark of Tonka Corporation for its pouncing spider game and game equipment. U.S. Patent Pending.

SWINGING SNAKES™

Company
Parker Brothers
Art Director
Karen Schmidt
Designer
Mitch Hyatt, Karen Schmidt
Illustrator
Mitch Hyatt
Photographer
Geoff Stein

Package graphics is an air brush illustration. The most difficult aspect was determining what "magic" looks like. The rules art and mechanical were created in Adobe Illustrator.

Objective
Spin the spinner and hang different colored snakes on the magically suspended wheel. Keep carefully adding snakes until somebody breaks the magic spell, and sends all the snakes tumbling to the ground.

SWINGING SNAKES is a trademark of Tonka Corporation for its magic hanging wheel game and game equipment.

**SKILL &
ACTION GAMES**

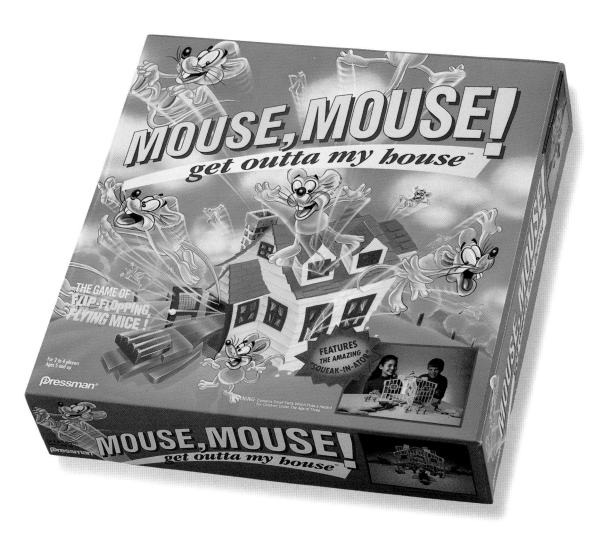

MOUSE, MOUSE! GET OUTTA MY HOUSE!™
Company
Pressman Toy Corp.
Design Firm
Wallace & Church
Photographer
Wilby Studios

Objective
Each player gets 5 funny-looking green mice in their part of the house. Get the mice out as fast as you can. Place one on your hand-flipper, push down, and off it goes. That meddlesome mouse will leap into the air with a SQUEAK! If you're lucky, he'll land in another player's house. Meanwhile, all the other players are sending mice every which way. The first player to have a mouseless house wins!

RING AROUND THE NOSY
Company
Pressman Toy Corp.
Design Firm
Bracchi Design
Photographer
Wilby Studios

Objective
Scoop up the rings with your trunk and win. Spread the rings out anywhere on the game board and get ready for hilarious fun. Players put their elephant masks on their hands behind their backs. Now dip your head low and scoop up a ring. The first one is easy, so try for another. The first player to get all three color rings on their trunk wins.

**SKILL &
ACTION GAMES**

TUBA - RUBA™
Company
Milton Bradley
Art Director
Jim Bremer
Designer
Jim Bremer, Erik Ela
Illustrator
Sharon Knettel

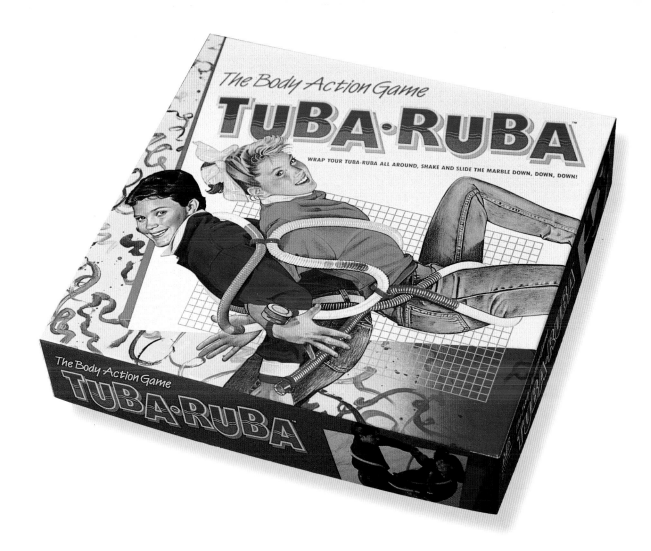

SIDEWINDER™
Company
Parker Brothers
Art Director/Designer
Steve Krupsky
Illustrator
William Rieser

The product illustration was created in Adobe Photoshop and saved as TIFF images that were later streamlined and brought into Adobe Illustrator. The entire package was output electronically.

Objective
This zigzag race to the top is a gravity-defying challenge of skill and speed. Force your marbles to climb up — up — up your ramp and drop off the top, into your rival's tray. But hurry! Your opponent is doing the same and his marbles are filling up your tray! You can even adjust the ramp's slope to "handicap" one player — or increase the marble-racing challenge. Who'll be first to get rid of all the marbles — and win?

SIDEWINDER is a trademark of Tonka Corporation for its uphill marble race game. U.S. Patent Pending.

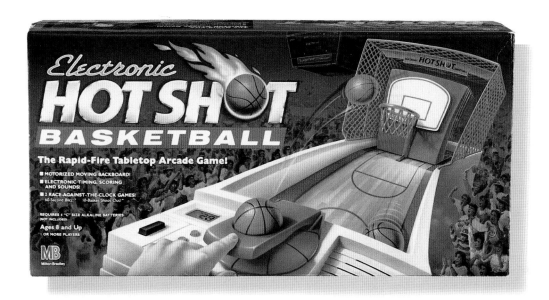

ELECTRONIC HOT SHOT® BASKETBALL
Company
Milton Bradley
Art Director/Designer
Jim Bremer
Illustrator
Rick Grayson

Objective
Choose from two exciting ways to play:
Score the most points in a minute or sink 10
baskets in the least amount of time. Since
the backboard is constantly moving, lining
up your shot can be a real challenge.

W® ,Wilson® and Hotshot® are registered trademarks which
distinguish the fine products of Wilson Sporting Goods Co.

WEAPONS AND WARRIORS™
Company
Pressman Toy Corp.
Design Firm
Wallace & Church
Photographer
Wilby Studios

One of 3 packages with family
look.

Objective
WEAPONS AND WARRIORS
brings the heroic Middle
Ages to life as players face
off in an action-packed
fight to the finish! Each
set features realistically
detailed weapons,
each designed for a
particular attack on
a defense. Roll
the battle dice
to see how
many steps
closer to the
enemy you can
bring your
soldiers and
weapons. Then
take aim and fire!
The first player to
wipe out the
opposing army
wins! All **WEAPONS
& WARRIORS** sets
can be combined for
the biggest battle of all.

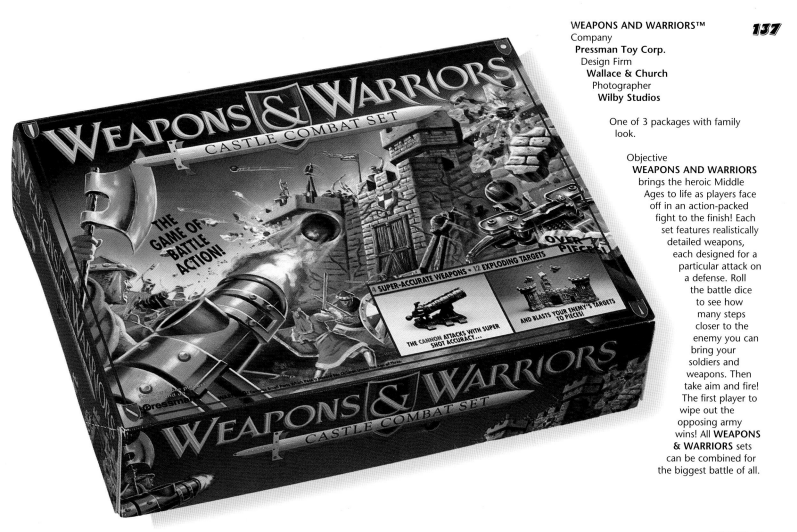

BANDU™
Company
Milton Bradley
Art Director
Jim Bremer
Designer
Jim Bremer, Erik Ela
Illustrator
David Schleinkoffer

Objective
Build your very own tower
from these odd-shaped wood
blocks and see if your
structure can outlast that of
your opponents. Using your
valuable BANDU Beans, bid
for the choice, stable pieces
or pay to avoid getting stuck
with those tough, hard-to-
place ones. But beware, once
you're out of beans, you're
out of luck! Pretty soon, each
turn becomes a breathtaking
balancing act, where a single
falling block from your tower
means...you're out, you've
been BANDU'ed!

138

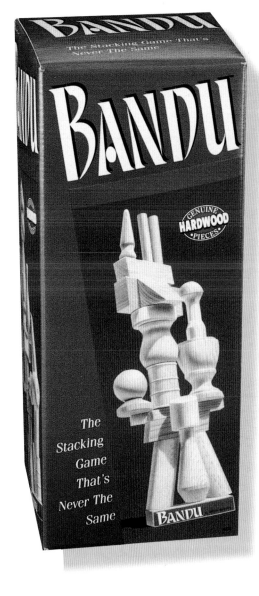

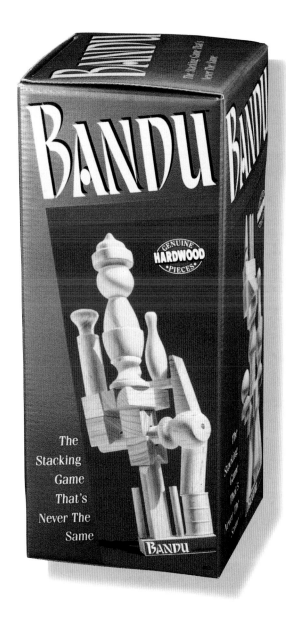

SCRAMBALL
Company
Milton Bradley
Art Director
Jim Bremer
Designer
Jim Bremer, Erik Ela
Illustrator
John Evans

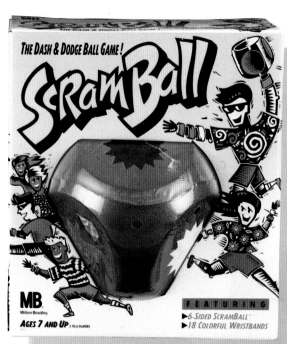

**DOMINO RALLY®
EXTREME ACTION SET**
Company
Pressman Toy Corp
Design Firm
Bracchi Design
Photographer
Wilby Studios

Objective
In the High Flying Hang Glider, a track of pivot dominoes leads up to the Big Mountain Launcher and releases the smooth-sailing glider. Watch it soar above the set-up that you've created. When a domino hits the wave, it sends the Wild Wind Surfer and his board up a full-tilt track. The surfer flips upside down and lands right-side up. The Mountain Bike Blast-Off is a triple stage stunt. The bike takes off on domino impact — flies through the Canyon — then blasts through the finish line.

TIPSY TOWER
Company
Milton Bradley Company
Art Director/Designer
Nan Finkenaur
Illustrator
Lon Busch
Photographer
Geoff Stein

Objective
Roll the die to find out on what color platform to place your next daredevil. Just be careful, for if you tip the tower, you have to keep all the daredevils that fall off. The steel ball rolling around in the base adds extra excitement, making TIPSY TOWER's balance even more precarious. The first player to place all of his or her daredevils on the TIPSY TOWER wins.

**SKILL &
ACTION GAMES**

SPLASH!
Company
E & M Games
Design Firm
Monnens-Addis Design
Art Director
Storey Jones
Designer
Debbie Smith
Illustrator
Lisa Berrett

Objective
An educational card game for ages 7 and up, **SPLASH!** is an aquatic educational game: the design of the cards depicts different sea characters. The cards are accompanied with educational copy about each particular sea animal. The bonus card, "Splash!," is represented by the mascot of the game — a dolphin.

GO FISH
Company
McGuire Toys Inc.
Designer
Richard McGuire
Photographer
Tony Centicola

141

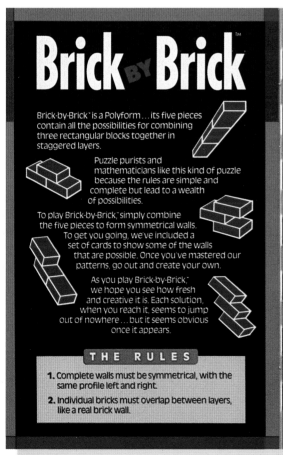

BRICK BY BRICK™
Company
Binary Arts Corporation
Art Director /Designer
Steve Wagner
Illustrator
Steve Wagner, Rusty Brough

Build over 60 puzzle shapes.

Objective
A puzzle to drive you up a wall.
Combine the 5 pieces to match
the puzzle shapes shown on the
enclosed cards, or invent your own.
Solutions are on the backs of cards.

NATURE'S SPACES™ (Set)
OCTOPUS PUZZLE™
Company
Binary Arts Corporation
All Design
Steve Wagner

Objective
Nature-theme puzzles, each different, each an
original puzzle design. Do they look simple?
Look out! Their challenge will surprise you.
Great for travel or stocking stuffers, for adults
as well as kids.

© Binary Arts Corp. 1993

142

NATURE'S SPACES™ (Set)
FROG POND™ PUZZLE™
Company
Binary Arts Corporation
All Design
Steve Wagner

© Binary Arts Corp. 1993

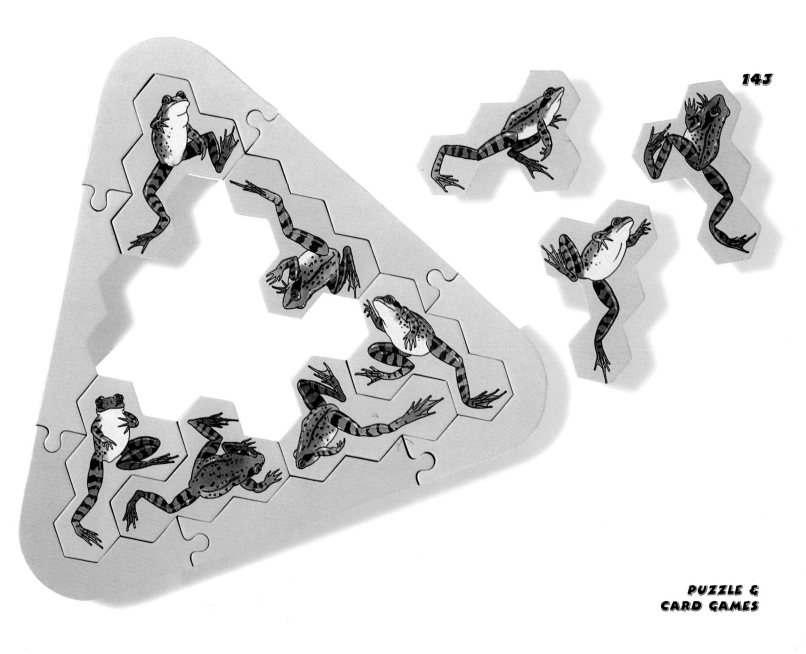

NATURE'S SPACES™ (Set)
BUTTERFLY PUZZLE™
Company
Binary Arts Corporation
All Design
Steve Wagner

144

NATURE'S SPACES™ (Set)
SNAKE PIT™ PUZZLE™
Company
Binary Arts Corporation
All Design
Steve Wagner

© Binary Arts Corp. 1993

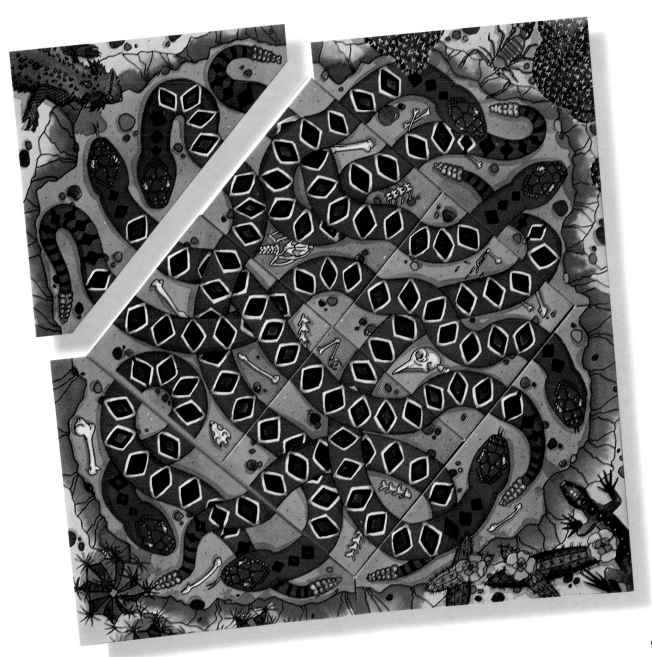

SPIN•OUT®
Company
Binary Arts Corporation
Art Director
Binary Arts
Designer
Binary Arts, Zane Carter

Object
A classic. Just turn the 7 disks, one by one. When the disks are all turned sideways, the slide will unlock and the puzzle is solved.

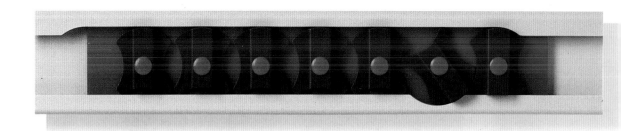

TOP•SPIN®
Company
Binary Arts Corporation
Art Director
Holger Burckhard, Zane Carter, Binary Arts Corp.
Designer
Binary Arts In-House, Holger Burckhardt

Objective
The object is simple — just put the numbers in order. Slide the 20 tokens around the track. Flip the turnstile to rearrange them. Easy, until it comes to that last number.

Just Match the Colors—Front and Back!

BACK•SPIN®
Company
Binary Arts Corporation
Art Director
Binary Arts
Designer
Holger Burckhardt, Binary Arts Corp.

Objective
A front and back, match – the – colors brainteaser. Scramble the balls front to back and up and down. Solve by putting the balls back in matching order.

SWITCHBACK™
Company
Binary Arts Corporation
Art Director
Steve Wagner, Binary Arts In-House
Designer
Holger Burckhardt, Steve Wagner
Illustrator
Steve Wagner

Objective
Arrange the colored balls to match one of the included puzzle patterns. Move balls across the playing field by shifting the 8 slider bars and tipping the game back and forth. You'll need a steady hand and a master plan to maneuver to the intended destinations.

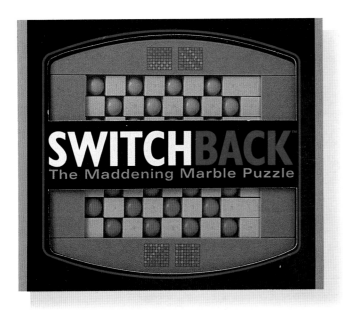

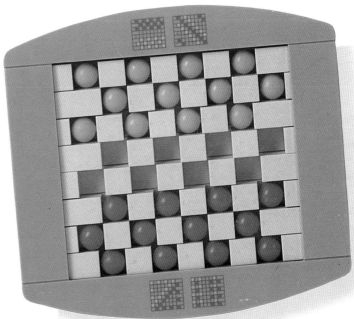

IZZI™
Company
Binary Arts Corporation
Art Director
Frank Nichols/Binary Arts Corporation
Designer
Frank Nichols

Objective
Just create a big square using the 64 cards. The only rule: touch black to black and white to white. Plays over and over. With almost a zillion solutions it's never the same game twice.

IZZI 2™
Company
Binary Arts Corporation
Art Director
Steve Wagner
Designer
Frank Nichols
Illustrator
Frank Nichols

Objective
Combine 12 colorful tiles to build 30 geometric puzzles. The only rules: touch red to red, blue to blue, green to green and yellow to yellow.

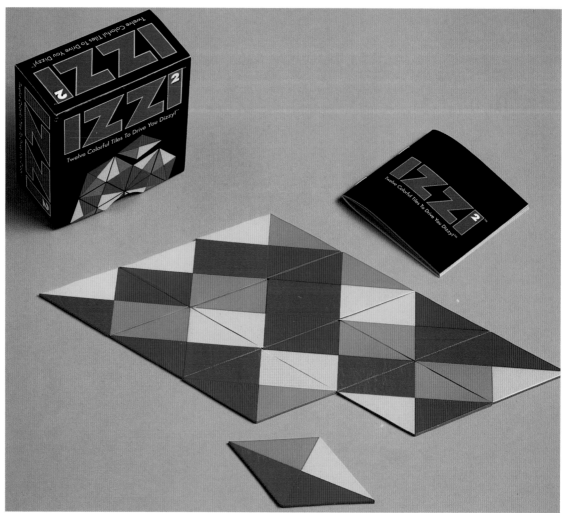

**PUZZLE &
CARD GAMES**

CUBITS™
Company
Binary Arts Corporation
All Design
Steve Wagner

Objective
Select a puzzle pattern from the challenge booklet. Then combine Cubits 16 pieces to match the puzzle pattern.

OSKAR'S CUBE™
Company
Crystal Lines, PL Australia
All Design
Crystal Lines

Objective
An ingenious 3-D maze. Really quite simple, until you realize that you must solve 3 mazes simultaneously to reach your goal.

PUZZLEHEAD
Company
McGuire Toys Inc.
Designer
Richard McGuire
Photographer
Tony Centicola

**BEVERLY HILLS, 90210™
CARD GAME**
Company
Milton Bradley
Art Director/Designer
Kiaran O'Brien

Objective
Collect your favorite characters
from the TV series and see who
ends up with the cards featuring
numbers from that famous zip
code, 90210. You get a point for
each zip code card you win. Or
you can try to completely avoid
getting any zip code cards for
special points.

GOLF LINE PUZZLE™
Company
Binary Arts Corporation
All Design
Steve Wagner

Objective
Combine 20 cards to build a bird's-eye view of one of the toughest golf courses you'll ever play.

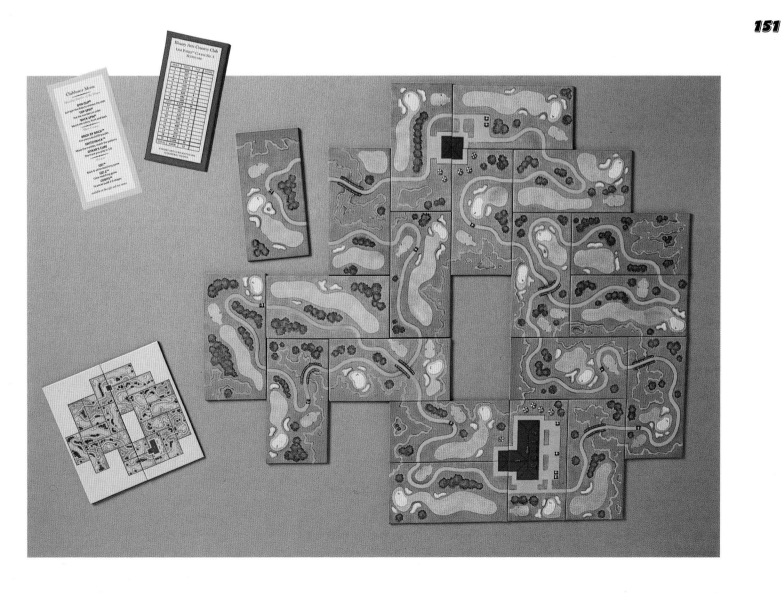

PENTOMINOES
Company
Binary Arts Corporation
All Design
Steve Wagner

Objective
Combine 12 different pieces to build dozens of puzzle shapes in this classic game based on 5 squares. Contains 2 puzzle sets and puzzle challenge booklet.

152

SNOWFLAKE™
Company
Binary Arts Corporation
Art Director
Steve Wagner
Designer
Steve Wagner, Stuart Coffin
Illustrator
Steve Wagner

Objective
Build a blizzard of shapes from ten hexagon-based pieces. Created by famed puzzler, Stuart Coffin, this gem is an avalanche of challenge.

MYSTERY SHAPES™
Company
Binary Arts Corporation
Designer/Illustrator
Steve Wagner

Brain-children of Dutch
puzzle wizard Oskar van
Deventer.

Objective
Each shape has 6 pieces
and just one solution.
Figure out how to build
all 4.

154

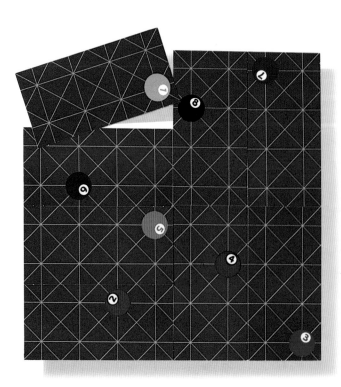

CRYPTIC CLASSICS:
SADDLE THE HORSES,
POSITION THE
POOLBALLS,
FIND THE ESCAPEE,
MAKE AN ELEPHANT
Company
Crystal Lines, PL Australia
Art Director
Crystal Lines, Dugald Keith
Designer
Crystal Lines, Dugald Keith
Illustrator
Bambi Smyth

Objective
**SADDLE THE HORSES, MAKE AN ELEPHANT, POSITION
THE POOL BALLS, FIND THE ESCAPEE:** Four classic puzzlers, revisited.
Place 3 cowboys on their broncos. Build an elephant picture, by combining
7 silhouettes. Place 8 pool balls properly in an 8 x 8 square. Make a
prisoner vanish. If you're stumped, a sealed solution is provided.

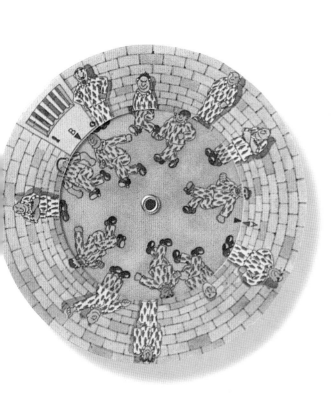

**PUZZLE &
CARD GAMES**

PARADOX 3-D JIGSAW PUZZLES
Company
Crystal Lines, PL Australia
Art Director
Crystal Lines, Dugald Keith
Designer
Crystal Lines, Dugald Keith
Illustrator
Bambi Smyth

Build foreground, middleground, and background puzzles to make one 3-D picture. Beware — each layer hides objects below!

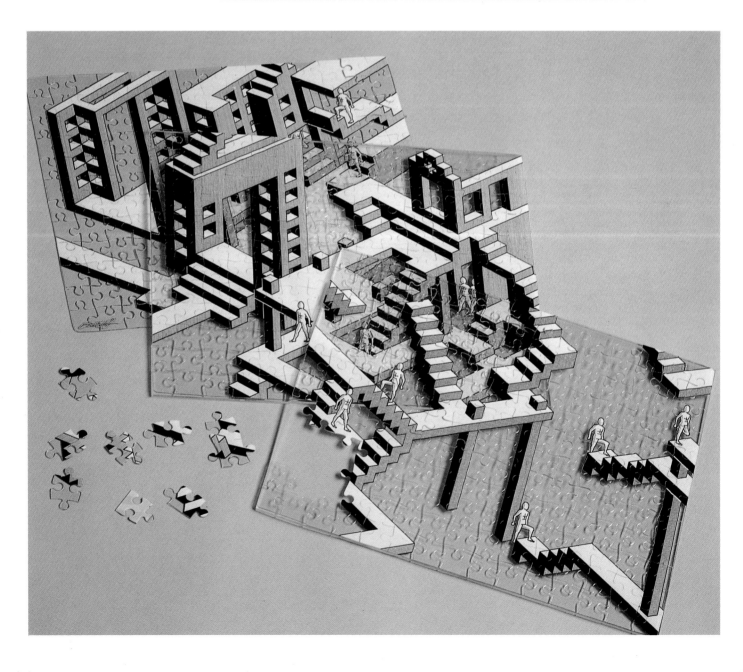

AMERICAN GRANDEUR
Company
Crystal Lines, PL Australia
Art Director
Crystal Lines, Dugald Keith
Designer
Crystal Lines, Dugald Keith
Illustrator
Bambi Smyth

Three layer jigsaw puzzle of a
nature scene.

INDEX

13 Dead End Drive	80
20 Questions® Nature And Science	123
1942: The Pacific Air War	39
A Day In The Life	78
Addams Family® Values	24
Aero The Acro•Bat™ Sega™	15
Alcon™	40
Alphabet Soup®	127
American Grandeur	157
Ants In The Pants®	110
Arch Rival®	90
Ashes Of Empire™	55
Ask Zandar	106
Astro Chase 3D™	43
Australian Rails	87
Back Off! Buzzard™	106
Back•Spin®	147
Baffles	83
Bandu™	138
Battleclash™	8
Beakman's World	107
Beverly Hills, 90210™	125
Beverly Hills, 90210™ Card Game	150
Bimini Run™	25
Blast Out™	131
Blurt!™	72
B.O.B.	11
Boggle® Jr. Letters	108
Boggle® Jr. Numbers	108
Bonjour Provence!	53
Bonkers	73
Bottle Topps®	97
Brain Quest™	119
Brick By Brick™	141
British Rails	87
Broadsides	75
Bubble Bobble™	52
The Bugs Bunny™ Crazy Castle	18
Bugs Bunny™ Rabbit Rampage	17

California Classics – 2. Go!	88
Carrollton	84
Casino Royale	101
Celebrity Taboo®	92
Chinese Chess	79
Clue®	76
Clue® – Little Detective™	124
Clue® – The Great Museum Caper	79
Congo's Caper	19
C.P.U. Bach	42
Crackers In My Bed®	127
Crocodile Dentist™	133
Cryptic Classics –	
Find The Escapee	155
Make An Elephant	155
Position The Poolballs	154
Saddle The Horses	154
Cubits™	149
Daffy Duck Game Boy™	56
Daffy Duck™ – The Marvin Missions	21
Dashin' Desperadoes™	16
The Death And Return Of Superman™	19
Déjà Vu™	18
Dennis The Menace™	114
Digger T. Rock™	14
Domino Rally® Extreme Action Set	139
Don't Get Rattled!™	130
Don't Panic®	102
Don't Wake Daddy®	102
Donut Disaster™	128
Dragonsphere	34
Dream On	69
Eat At Ralph's™	103
Eek! The Cat™	23
Electronic Hot Shot® Basketball	137
Elemento®	84
F-15 Strike Eagle III	28
Fleet Defender™	48
The Flintstones®	24

Flying Thunder	114
Forbidden Bridge	104
Future Stories	117
Game Boy™ Final Fantasy Legend	56
Game Boy™ Mousetrap Hotel	57
Game Boy™ Speedy Gonzales	57
Game Boy™ Super Scrabble®	57
Get Ahead Games –	
'Smath™	120
Spellway™	120
State The Facts™	120
Go Fish	140
Golf Line Puzzle™	151
Guesstures™	93
GunForce™	22
Headline Deadline	89
Hey Jazz Fish!	26
Hidden Talents™	116
The Humans	41
The Humans – Insult To Injury	33
Inside Paris	52
Interference/Nincompoop	89
In the Picture	104
Izzi™	148
Izzi 2™	148
Jack Sprats Table	105
Joe & Mac 2: Lost In The Tropics™	8
The Journeyman Project™	31
Jurassic Park™	7
Jurassic Park II™	21
Kids Games™—	
Goldilocks And The Three Bears	112
Little Red Riding Hood	112
Three Little Pigs	113
King's Table™	51
Laugh Factory	46
Les Vins De France™	100
Life Of The Party –	
The Coffee House Murder™	99

Passion Cabana In Havana™	98	Platter-O'-Fortune	88	Splat!™	109
Rockin' Late At The Prom Of '58™	98	pre•fix	65	Star Trek: The Next Generation®	
Who Killed Roger Ellington™	99	Prophecy: Viking Child™	45	Interactive VCR Board Game	59
Life Stories	74	Pirates! Gold®	36	Street Combat™	10
Looney Tunes Smush 'Em™	121	Play It By Ear	58	Super Baseball 2020™	9
Mac Attack	47	Play It By Ear 2	58	Super NES Play Action Football™	10
Mambopaint	47	Power Gladiators	58	Super R-Type®	20
Metal Combat™	18	Puzzlehead	150	Super Soccer	16
Mighty Max™	23	QIX™	29	Swinging Snakes™	134
Monopoly®	78	Rastan™	53	Switchback™	147
Monopoly® Anniversary	68	The Ren & Stimpy Show™–		Taboo™	92
Monopoly® Junior	124	*Buckeroos*	14	Tales Of The Crystals	62
Monopoly® Sega™	6	*Veediots!*	20	TIME – The Game	82
Monopoly Tin®	64	Renegade™	34	Tip The Cows!™	85
Mouse, Mouse!		Return Of The Phantom™	27	Tipsy Tower	139
Get Outta My House!™	135	Ring Around The Nosy	135	Top•Spin®	146
Mystery Shapes™	153	Risk®	66	Total Carnage™	22
Nature's Spaces™ –		Risky Woods™	12	Travel Buff®	95
Butterfly Puzzle™	144	Saved By The Bell™	122	Tribond®	70
Frog Pond Puzzle™	143	Scattergories®	91	Tribond®, Clue-Set Cards #2	70
Octopus Puzzle™	142	Scattergories® Junior	115	Tribond® Kids	129
Snake Pit™ Puzzle™	145	Scramball	138	Trivial Pursuit® Junior	128
NHL® Stanley Cup®	17	Secrets	100	True Colors™	97
Nippon Rails	86	The Shadow™	15	Tuba - Ruba™	136
Nomad™	35	Shadowgate™	13	Uncle Wiggily™	106
Noodle Goes To The Hospital	38	Shakin' Sorry®	83	Valkyrie™	44
North American Rails	86	Shamu™ – Protect Our Seas™ Game	118	Wafflin' Willy™	96
North And South™	7	Shark Attack® Bowling	110	Weapons And Warriors™	137
One By One	98	Sidewinder™	136	Where In The USA Is	
Operation Wolf®	54	Sid Meier's Civilization™	49	Carmen Sandiego?®	71
Oskar's Cube™	149	Sid Meier's Civil War™	44	Willie Go Boom™	118
Paradox 3-D Jigsaw Puzzles	156	Simon	56	Wipeout	125
Party Mania™	60	Sky Shark™	29	Word By Word	99
Pass The Pigs™	90	Sorry!®	68	Yahoo Buckeroo!™	122
Peanut Butter & Jelly™	126	Snardvark™	130	Your Dreams	88
Pentominoes	152	Snowflake™	152		
Perfection®	131	Spider Attack™	134		
Perpetual Notion	82	Spin•Out®	146		
Pie Face™	126	Splash!	140		